Understanding Victims of Interpersonal Violence

Understanding Victims of Interpersonal Violence: A Guide for Investigators and Prosecutors provides accessible information for criminal justice personnel "in the trenches" with victims of violence to aid in understanding and explaining their behavior.

This guide sheds light on interpersonal violence victims' decisions and actions by providing context and naming factors that commonly impact victim responses. These include internal factors such as culture, religion, shame, and personality, as well as external factors like access to services, support systems, and resources. These factors inhibit or facilitate responses like disclosure, resistance, and participation (or lack thereof) in the prosecution of the offenders. This book also explores the influence of the perpetrator, as well as more deeply examining victim responses that typically offer challenges to investigators and prosecutors; for example, continued contact with the offender, lack of resistance, and issues in disclosure. Finally, the guide provides concrete tools to assist investigators in interviewing and for prosecutors to use during the prosecutorial process.

This book is designed for investigators, prosecutors, advocates, criminal justice practitioners, and students of these subjects.

Veronique N. Valliere is a licensed psychologist and has her doctorate in Clinical Psychology from the Graduate School of Applied and Professional Psychology of Rutgers University. She has more than 25 years of experience in the field and has worked clinically with violent offenders and their victims, adult and child. She is the owner and director of Valliere & Counseling Associates, Inc., an outpatient treatment center for mental health and interpersonal violence, with offices that treat victims and offenders and provide consultation, training, expert witness services, and evaluations. She also serves on the Pennsylvania Sexual Offender Assessment Board and has been reappointed continuously since 1997. She has published on the topic of sexual assault and presented on the same at international, national, and local conferences. She has trained for the Federal Bureau of Investigation, U.S. Department of Justice (DOJ), U.S. Department of Defense (DOD), Bureau of Indian Affairs, Ontario Police, Alberta Crown Prosecutor's Office, Amber Alert, Army JAG Office, Pennsylvania State Parole, National Center for the Prosecution of Violence Against Women, and other agencies. She been a guest presenter at many forensic- and violence-related conferences. She is recognized as an expert on victim behavior and has testified nationally and internationally. She has testified before the U.S. Congress and Judiciary Committee regarding sexual assault in the military and has consulted with DOD and DOJ. She has been interviewed for a number of popular magazines on sexual assault and domestic violence, including *The New York Times*, *People*, *Self*, and *Good Housekeeping*. She has appeared on "PBS NewsHour," "CBS This Morning," and other programs and radio shows. Dr. Valliere was used as an expert in the sexual assault trial of Bill Cosby. In 2009, she established an annual conference on the investigation, prosecution, and treatment of violence, entitled "Right From the Start."

Understanding Victims of Interpersonal Violence

A Guide for Investigators and Prosecutors

Veronique N. Valliere

NEW YORK AND LONDON

First published 2020
by Routledge
52 Vanderbilt Avenue, New York, NY 10017

and by Routledge
2 Park Square, Milton Park, Abingdon, Oxon, OX14 4RN

Routledge is an imprint of the Taylor & Francis Group, an informa business

© 2020 Taylor & Francis

The right of Veronique N. Valliere to be identified as author of this work has been asserted by her in accordance with sections 77 and 78 of the Copyright, Designs and Patents Act 1988.

All rights reserved. No part of this book may be reprinted or reproduced or utilised in any form or by any electronic, mechanical, or other means, now known or hereafter invented, including photocopying and recording, or in any information storage or retrieval system, without permission in writing from the publishers.

Trademark notice: Product or corporate names may be trademarks or registered trademarks, and are used only for identification and explanation without intent to infringe.

Library of Congress Cataloging-in-Publication Data
Names: Valliere, Veronique N., author.
Title: Understanding victims of interpersonal violence : a guide
   for investigators and prosecutors / Veronique N. Valliere.
Description: New York, NY : Routledge, 2020. | Includes
   bibliographical references and index.
Identifiers: LCCN 2019031980 (print) | LCCN 2019031981
   (ebook) | ISBN 9780367422936 (hardback) | ISBN
   9781498780483 (paperback) | ISBN 9780367823245 (ebook)
Subjects: LCSH: Sexual abuse victims. | Victims of family
   violence. | Victims of violent crimes. | Criminal investigation. |
   Criminal justice, Administration of.
Classification: LCC HV6625 .V35 2020 (print) | LCC HV6625
   (ebook) | DDC 362.88—dc23
LC record available at https://lccn.loc.gov/2019031980
LC ebook record available at https://lccn.loc.gov/2019031981

ISBN: 978-0-367-42293-6 (hbk)
ISBN: 978-1-4987-8048-3 (pbk)
ISBN: 978-0-367-82324-5 (ebk)

Typeset in Sabon
by Apex CoVantage, LLC

This book is dedicated to my husband, family, and staff who all believed in this book, especially Barb who made me do it. Additionally, it is dedicated to the prosecutors I have worked with, who have taught me so much and persist in the mission of justice. Mostly, it is dedicated to the courageous victims who have educated me on their wisdom.

Contents

Acknowledgements	xii
Introduction	1

SECTION I
Victim Response to Interpersonal Violence   **5**

1   Victim Response to Assault: Is It "Counterintuitive" Behavior?   7

What Is "Counterintuitive" Behavior? Is There Such a Thing? 9
Persistence of Myths About Assault 10
When Rape Meets the Myth 13
What Are the Facts? 13
Why Do I Need to Know This? 14
Summary 15
References 16

2   "I Was in Shock:" Internal Factors Impacting Victim Response   18

Fear 19
  Emotional Impact of Fear 19
  Physiological Impact of Fear 19
Cognitive Biases and Unexpected Decisions 20
  Loss Aversion 21
  Confirmation Bias: "See, I Told You He Wasn't Like That" 22
  Familiarity and Perception of Risk 23

viii Contents

Personal Control, Fear, and Risk 24
Habituation 25
Personalization of Risk 25
Culture and Religion 26
  *Culture: "That's Normal for Them; It's a Cultural
    Thing" 27*
  Religion: "But God Says . . ." 28
Beliefs and Values 29
  *It's a "Just World" or What Goes Around, Comes
    Around 30*
  Rape Myth Acceptance and Rape Scripts 31
*Confusion About or Failure to Identify the Assault
  or Abuse 32*
  Relationship to the Perpetrator 33
  Alcohol Use 35
  Absence of Force or Violence 35
Blame, Shame, and Guilt 37
Vulnerability and Weakness 38
Prior History of Abuse/Assault 39
Socialization to Aggression and Conflict 42
Fear of Penalization 43
Summary 45
References 46

**3 "Where Was I Supposed to Go?" External Factors That
Influence Victim Response and Help-Seeking**   **49**

Access to Services 49
Barriers to Help-Seeking During the Offense 51
  Presence or Protection of Witnesses/Children 53
  Opportunity for Escape 54
  *Experience With and Revictimization by the Law
    Enforcement or the Criminal Justice System 54*
Consequences of Reporting 57
  Consequences to Others/Offender 57
  Retaliation 59
  Loss 60
Societal Messages 60
Support System of Victim 61
Other Post-Offense Influences on Victim Response 63
Summary 64
References 65

Contents   ix

4 "I Will Not Be Denied:" Influence of the Offender on
  Victim Behavior   68

  Influence on the Victim 69
    *Getting the Victim to Cooperate: Why Did She Allow
      It? 70*
    Identifying and Exploiting Vulnerability 71
    Building Attachment 72
    Being Nice 73
    Promising to Change: Creating Hope 74
    Creating Confusion by Acting Normal 75
    *"Grooming" or Preparing the Victim to Be a
      Victim 76*
    Past Experience With the Offender 78
  Influence of the Offender on the Community 79
    Creating the Public Persona 80
    Controlling the Information 81
    *Creating a Victim's Reputation and Setting Up
      Retaliation 81*
    Deception After the Disclosure 82
  Summary 83
  References 84

5 "I Should Have Kicked His Ass:" Male Victims of Intimate
  Violence   85

  *"Be a Man:" Traditional Masculinity and Societal
    Messages 86*
  Having a Penis 87
  Shame and Stigma 89
  Victim Blaming 89
  Minimization of Assault 90
  Access to Services 91
  Summary 91
  References 92

SECTION 2
Common Types of Victim Responses   95

6 "What Was I Supposed to Say?" Issues in Disclosures
  of Assault   97

  General Issues to Remember About Memory 98

x Contents

Delayed Disclosure 100
Types of Disclosure and the Process of Telling 101
  Interactional Component of Disclosure 102
  Trauma and Disclosure 104
Triggers for Disclosure 104
  Opportunity and Social Support 104
  Increased Needs of the Victim 105
  Increased Knowledge of the Victim 105
  *Removal From the Perpetrator or Changes in the
    Abuser's Behavior 106*
Trauma and Memory 106
Recantation 108
Secondary Victimization as a Result of Disclosure 109
Summary 110
References 111

7 **"But I Love Him:" Continued Contact With the Offender** **114**

Relationships as the Weapon of the Offender 114
  Access to the Victim 115
  Provides Excuses and Explanations for the Abuse 116
  Used Against the Victim 117
  Establishes Status Issues 118
*Why Doesn't She Leave? The Meaning of the Relationship
  to the Victim 119*
  Practical Matters 119
  Confusion and Disbelief About the Act and Actor 120
  Wants to Be Normal and Safe Again 121
  Loves the Offender and Fears the Loss 122
  Thinks the Danger Can Be Controlled 122
  Danger 123
Suggestions for Interviews 124
Summary 125
References 126

8 **"Nah, I'm Good:" Understanding Victim Resistance** **128**

Let's Just Talk: Verbal Resistance 129
Tie Them Really Tight: Nonverbal Resistance 131
Freeze, Flight, or Fight 132
  Freeze 132
  Flight 134

Fight 136
Barriers to Resistance 137
Children or Protection of Others 137
Prior History of Abuse 138
Inability to Resist 138
Summary 139
References 140

9 "Commit to Courage:" Conclusions and Suggestions   **142**

Appendix A: Questions Instead of "Why?"   146
Appendix B: Sample Voir Dire Questions   150
Appendix C: Interviewing Victims for Sentencing   154
Index   157

Acknowledgements

Despite my years of work with victims and offenders, I could not have ever appreciated the challenges and commitment of the passionate, dedicated, and relentless prosecutors, advocates, and trainers that I have been privileged to train beside and be mentored by, especially regarding what victims face through the investigation and prosecution process. I have learned a great deal about the decision-making that goes into the process, how investigators and prosecutors can suffer alongside the victims, and how the system can be thankless, from the top down to the bottom up. Each time I would become stalled or question the need for this writing, I would encounter a new prosecutor hungry for this information or another case that fell because of the lack of education on these matters.

In particular, I would like to acknowledge Bridget Ryan, Esq., who taught me, supported me, and gave me fantastic ideas throughout my journey. She has an unending passion for addressing injustice to victims and uses this to motivate her continual education and support of young prosecutors, making a profound difference in the work and world. I would like to thank my husband and partner, Rodney Schulz, for continually supporting my work, my mission, and my writing, as well as giving me an "outsider's" opinion on my thoughts and beliefs, challenging me to explain something more clearly or succinctly. My staff has been encouraging throughout and has made it possible for me to write while keeping the practice going. I could not have done this without you.

There have been many before me who have made the foundation on which this book has been built. The attorneys, advocates, and experts I have worked with at PCAR, APRI, and Aequitas all contributed to my knowledge and commitment. Thank you especially Joyce Lukima, Hon. Doug Miles, Jen Markowitz, Rob Stelle, J. R. Waltemyer, Sandy Tullius, Barbara Knox, and many, many others in field who continue to strive to make things better and have given me many opportunities to make myself better in it.

Introduction

Because if the girl was lying, our lives could go on as usual.
—F. Bachman, Beartown

The week I knew I was going to write this book, I spent every day dealing with the issues I hope to address in it. On Monday, I flew back from a training of prosecutors, where I showed videos of convicted sexual offenders describing how they influenced, manipulated, and controlled their victims and others whom they convinced they could "never do a thing like that." On Tuesday, I worked with victims. One was a survivor of domestic violence, who the week before had had to deal with a coworker describing what a "great guy" her ex-husband was and what good work he did for them. The man had been in treatment as well and had admitted some of his behavior, explaining how he "had to act that way" (controlling, demeaning) because his wife was crazy, maybe even bipolar, and needed direction and management. Another woman had been sexually assaulted by her teacher as a teen—even in the classroom during class, having had to masturbate him under the desk while he pretended to work with her. She never told anyone until adulthood and still struggled with the impact her abuse had had on her life and relationships, as well as on her body, which still suffers from the trauma.

Wednesday was even more disappointing. I was involved in a trial in which a five-year-old boy disclosed to his pediatrician that his "daddy was teaching him bad things." The boy was brought to the doctor because he was putting his finger in his anus and rectum and eating the feces he picked out. He also picked at and rubbed his genitals. When the doctor explored what these "bad things" were, he said his daddy was putting his "pee pee" in the boy's "butt." The case went unfounded because the boy would not repeat his disclosures to Child Protective Services investigators. Six months later, following a visit with his father, the child returned distraught, reporting that another assault had happened to him that weekend. He repeated the disclosure to the pediatrician, this

2 Introduction

time in front of an investigator, elaborating on the abuse and behavior of his father. The child was deemed credible and the father was "indicated" for abuse of the child. The finding was not appealed or challenged by the father; however, the allegations occurred during a custody battle. There was no medical evidence of anal penetration, something the pediatrician testified about during the hearing for a protection order. She repeatedly stated to the judge that the research demonstrates that medical findings or evidence in confirmed sexual abuse cases are extremely rare, even with anal penetration, explaining how elastic the rectum and anus are in order to accommodate stool. She also said that the most important evidence of abuse, according to research of confirmed abuse, is the consistent and credible disclosures of the victim. Despite this, and despite testimony about how testifying in front of a perpetrator can cause a victim to recant or minimize abuse out of fear of the perpetrator, the judge had the child testify on the stand. He couldn't, so the parents were removed from the courtroom. The child, after encouragement, then told the judge and attorneys that his father scratched his "butt with a twig from a branch outside" and denied that he had made allegations of anal rape. The father got supervised visitations beginning immediately for three months, based on the fact that there was no medical evidence of anal trauma a day or more after the assault.

On Thursday, I evaluated a mother whose paramour had been convicted of sexually assaulting their daughter, pled guilty, and served his sentence, which included participation in sexual offender treatment. Child protection was involved in the family again because of emotional and verbal abuse by the father (who had returned to the home with children after his incarceration) toward the youngest child, who became suicidal and ran away because of the abuse. During his evaluation, the father admitted to much of the abuse, which was highly sexualized in content. The mother was clear that she did not believe her son or her daughter, eventually blowing up in the interview with me. She began yelling,

> *I don't care what no one says! I don't believe anything. Tell me this—if he did this, why would Joey call and say he missed his dad? Huh? And no one is going to make me consider that Adam 'sexually abused' anyone. You know, that kid, we couldn't keep her away from the pornography when she was that age that she said he did stuff to her. What kind of girl at 13 wants to see her dad's porn? And if she is so 'traumatized' by her father, why did she go get knocked up? Want to explain that? The system poisoned my children and I don't care what anyone says. I'm not listening to no one. He just took the guilty plea because he has a high gravity score—he explained it all to me. He couldn't afford no 30–50 years in prison, that's why he said he did it!*

The interview ended. The woman's daughter had been diagnosed with post-traumatic stress disorder (PTSD) and was not in contact with her mother. The woman stated that Adam had beaten her early in their relationship, but they had "gotten through it." The children had been in and out of foster care because of their parents' addiction and instability. I never got to help this woman understand her children, or help her family, or learn to live with a convicted sexual offender without endangering herself or children.

On Friday, I went to court to testify about how a man convicted of sexually abusing a small girl met the legal criteria for classification as a sexually violent predator. He was previously convicted of having a knife on school property, cutting up a man's face with a razor blade, wearing a ski mask and robbing someone at knifepoint, and assaulting and masturbating in front of a friend's older mother four years prior. The child reported being abused for four years, including vaginal penetration. She was able to describe how it "started off soft and then got hard" and how sometimes "cream" came out of his penis. She told investigators how scared she was of the perpetrator, who she said threatened to kill her turtle and eat him. The child said she did tell her mother, who confronted the perpetrator. When the perpetrator denied the abuse, the mother told the child she did not believe her. The mother was also mentally and cognitively limited, providing little support for the child. During my testimony that the man was a violent predator, the defense attorney focused on the charge that the man pled to, only admitting to evidence that he had grabbed the child's genitals and forced the child's hand on his penis (not the other 80-plus charges he faced). After I explained that convictions rarely reflected what actually happened, he confronted me with the fact that the child once recanted the allegations. I explained that I was not surprised, especially when faced with the fact her mother did not believe her. The week ended with the man being declared a sexually violent predator by the judge. But when I got home, I had an email about another case: a decision limiting my testimony to why a victim will not resist an assault and disallowing the other testimony because it is "common knowledge" that victims do not disclose abuse. I wish that were true.

This is a true, if paraphrased, recounting of the week. I will do this throughout the book, changing names, but not facts. Although this week was especially replete with examples of why this book will be useful, it is not extremely unusual. I am a clinical and forensic psychologist whose specialty is interpersonal violence. I treat and assess victims and perpetrators of violence. I have treated hundreds of victims, child and adult, as well as interviewed, evaluated, or treated thousands of offenders. What follows is what I have learned from the research, my work with victims, and my work with perpetrators, who are an excellent source of information on how they exploit our misunderstanding,

4 Introduction

misinformation, and faulty expectations of victims and perpetrators in the context of private violence.

Offenders continue to succeed, co-opting us and the victims to help them. Even offenders who have been convicted and are on registries are succeeding. Just recently in my community, a registered sexual offender who was on parole and being managed, was found naked in a hotel room with two small girls. He had convinced their mothers he had changed and had offered to babysit so the moms could "have a night out." He presented to others as harmless and disabled. He was getting all we had to give regarding supervision, notification, and treatment. And yet . . .

And people are angry. We hate the confusion, helplessness, and fear that interpersonal violence creates. We want answers, we want syndromes, we want to be able to tell by looking who is a good guy and who is a bad guy. Most good people want knowledge to protect their children. Those who can't are filled with shame and fear of finding out they failed their children and didn't know the offender. When victims haven't been able to help us catch an offender or protect them, when offenders are "good" guys who look like us and whom we trusted, we are scared. We would rather deny than face that offenders are among us, exploiting us, tricking us, and succeeding. It seems that is easier to believe that victims will lie rather than that we cannot clearly identify perpetrators and prevent assault.

What I hope to offer in this book is easy-to-understand explanations of victim response to violence and practical ways to explain, explore, and reveal these responses. This is not intended to be a book of tricks, but a book of tools to help expose the offenders and their techniques, as well as to make the victims' behaviors make sense in the context of the abuse. The more we can understand and explain victim response, the more our system can focus on the real issue—prosecuting offenders rather than defending or demonizing victims.

Section I

Victim Response to Interpersonal Violence

Chapter 1

Victim Response to Assault
Is It "Counterintuitive" Behavior?

The behavior detailed within (police interviews) was inconsistent with a person who had been sexually assaulted," Castor testified during Cosby's second court appearance. "Her actions, on her own, including going to a lawyer before going to police, had created a credibility issue for her that could never be improved upon.
—Paquette, D., The Washington Post, *February 2, 2016*

On April 15, 2013, at 2:49 p.m., runners in the Boston Marathon were determinedly running toward the finish line when two homemade bombs exploded, killing three people and injuring 260 more. Pictures of the scene show the victims wandering in the street, frozen still or running away. Photos show first responders running toward the blast. News coverage captured a wide array of responses to the tragedy.

That day, and in the days following, the community gathered around the victims. Boston residents coined the term "Boston Strong" to capture the resilience of the town, the commitment to get "back to normal." The next day, people visited the blast site, filled with shock and questions of "why?" Runners completed mini-marathons in their cities and towns. The nation supported the victims and were focused on the acts of the perpetrators.

What is almost as important as what happened in response to the Boston Marathon bombing is what did not happen. No one blamed the victims. No one questioned why the victims wanted to run, why they didn't run faster or slower, or whether they would ever run again. The "return to normal" of Boston was celebrated as strength and was not used to minimize the event. No one said, "Well, if it was that bad, how did they go to work the next day?" No one disputed the potential impact, regardless of the victims' behaviors. No one thought it was crazy to visit the bombing site. Regarding the perpetrators, no one made excuses. No one said, "Boys will be boys." It was not considered a joke, explained away by alcohol, or considered a mistake or accident.

I use this example to illustrate that we have clarity, as a community, regarding victim responses and perpetrator behaviors in tragic events like this. However, we lose this clarity when it comes to interpersonal violence and assault. Concerning sexual assault, according to the most recent available data from the National Crime Victimization Survey (Truman & Morgan, 2016), out of 1,000 sexual assaults, *only 344 are reported to police.* Of those, 63 lead to arrest and even fewer are referred for prosecution. Estimates indicate that of 1,000 sexual assaults, only six offenders are incarcerated (Federal Bureau of Investigation, 2015). Recent research by Dr. Campbell and colleagues at Michigan State University found that sexual assault case attrition happens very early in the investigation and prosecution process. In fact, through studying 12 years of data from law enforcement, she found that 86% of reported sexual assaults never went further than the police (Campbell, 2012). Law enforcement simply did not refer the reports to prosecutors. These same issues appear in cases involving domestic violence and child abuse as well.

At least some of the explanation for this failure was the victim's behavior and reaction during and following the crime and the ignorance of investigators about victim behavior. The victim faces blame and judgement from the very beginning of the investigation and prosecution process. This contributes to the failure to pursue investigation, as well as the traumatization of the victim by the process. A victim who is unsupported or who feels judged or mistreated by law enforcement is unlikely to be cooperative, even if the case is referred to prosecutors. After disclosing, countless victims have told me and others, "I wish I never told. This is worse than the rape itself." I have asked audiences of attorneys, law enforcement, and advocates if they would go through the system themselves or would recommend their loved ones pursue prosecution of rape. Very few people raised their hands. One recent study demonstrated that more than 80% of surveyed police officers overestimated rates of false allegations (Mennicke, Anderson, Oehme, & Kennedy, 2014), a finding that has clear implications for interview, investigation, and treatment of victims reporting rape.

In our ongoing attempts to understand the success of perpetrators of violence and abuse, we often focus on the victim as opposed to the offenders. Whether it is victim blaming or the scrutiny of "counterintuitive" victim behavior in response to an assault, we look to the victim to give us answers or understanding. If a child does not act afraid of the abuser, perhaps the abuse did not happen. If the wife continues to love the violent husband, maybe something is wrong with her. If the rape victim does not run and scream, maybe it wasn't really rape, but "buyer's remorse." Those audience members understand the scrutiny and judgement victims face. Understanding and communicating the logic of victim behavior is the duty of all of us through the process of prosecution.

What Is "Counterintuitive" Behavior? Is There Such a Thing?

In the criminal justice arena, victim behaviors are often referred to as "counterintuitive" or " nonintuitive" behaviors. This is not a diagnostic or psychological term. It refers to behaviors or responses that are evaluated by others as behaviors by the victim that are not "real" victim behaviors. We have projected expectations of how a victim would or should react if he or she was "really" assaulted. When a victim does not react in expected ways, that victim's behaviors can be used to "prove" his or her lack of credibility (cited in Long, 2007). In fact, Long (2007) points out that if the victim's behavior does not fit expectations, that behavior is easily used to create doubt about the victim's experience or report of the assault. What is "real" is that victim response to sexual assault is so varied, research has yet to prove there is a set of expected responses, resulting in the disproving of "syndrome" evidence (for example, battered woman's syndrome or rape trauma syndrome) (Ellison, 2005; Dutton, 2009). In fact, even the use of the term "counterintuitive" has been criticized as reinforcing these problematic beliefs and assumptions (Fanflik, 2007).

Some of the more typical examples of behavior that are considered counterintuitive include an array of behaviors that are fairly common to victims both during and after the offense. This includes a failure to disclose; inconsistent or piecemeal disclosure; failure to forcibly resist an assault; failing to escape when an opportunity presents itself; having continued contact with the offender, even including consensual sex; or acting "normal" following a sexual or physical assault.

In fact, there is no such thing as "counterintuitive" victim behavior. All victims respond to assault in individualized ways, though many show similar behaviors. No singular study will predict how a victim will act or will prove that the response means that the victim has been abused. No model predicts how victims will cope with assault, as victim responses are determined by an array of factors—internal and external (Littleton & Breitkopf, 2006). What we do know, in fact, is that the overarching belief that victims will or should react a certain way in an assault is a significant factor in preventing a victim from reporting. It also contributes to victim blaming in interpersonal violence.

Even though there is no "typical" response to violence, investigators, prosecutors, judges, juries, and defense attorneys often rely on using victim responses to judge victim credibility or offender culpability. Long, Kristiansson, and Mallios (2013) wrote, "these fallacies have been reinforced for centuries by public discourse, inadequate laws created by misguided and uneducated legislators, and the various defense strategies designed to discredit victims by the exploitation of common rape myths." Faulty expectations not only contribute to victim blaming and using the victim's behavior against him or her, they contribute to the failure of the criminal justice system to expose the offender and hold him accountable. When laypeople rely on myths and misinformation, they may be prone to inaccurately label a victim as not credible, to minimize the offenses, and to dismiss the victim's allegations and testimony about violence.

Persistence of Myths About Assault

These faulty expectations are formed in large part by the internalization of misinformation about assault, media portrayals of victims, and a lack of understanding about human behavior (or at least a failure to apply our knowledge). Typically, people create scenarios of how they would react in the face of an act that they think is extreme, tragic, or terrible, like sexual assault or intimate partner violence. "I would kick him in the balls," "if he ever touched me, I would leave right away," or "I would never allow that to happen," are the types of statements made by people who do not have the experience or understanding of being assaulted, especially of being assaulted by someone known to them.

What are some of the myths that persist about sexual assault and domestic violence? For sexual assault, a "real" rape would include a stranger, force, injury, a weapon, and an "innocent" or unsuspecting victim. Perhaps someone who is assaulted while jogging or locking up her business or by someone who breaks into her home. These crimes hypothetically draw a clear line between victim and perpetrator and between right and wrong, and indicate who is to blame. However, statistics show that even these crimes produce unanticipated victim responses. For example, in 2014, an average of only 50% of violent sexual assaults by strangers were reported to law enforcement, according to the U.S. Bureau of Justice Statistics (Planty & Langton, 2016). The same survey also reveals that more than 80% of both violent and sexual assaults were committed by those known to the victim.

Some of the information we know about sexual assault seems as though it should now be part of society's common knowledge. I was confronted once by an attorney who asked, "come on—doesn't everyone watch 'Law and Order: SVU?'" Despite more discussion and media portrayals of sexual assault and domestic violence, research demonstrates that myths and misinformation still significantly impact the community's evaluation of and understanding of assault. In fact, the media still tends to highlight the more dramatic, stereotypical stories of abuse and rape. In a recent study, men continued to endorse hostile rape myths toward men and women. These included overt victim blaming and stereotyping; for example, "if he were a real man, he wouldn't have let himself get raped" or "she was a bad girl and deserved it." Both women and men endorsed what the authors called "benevolent" rape myths toward women (Davies,

Gilston, & Rogers, 2012). These myths included subtle blaming of the victim by identifying the victims' choices, like drinking or "getting herself into that situation," or indirectly, as holding her responsible for the sexual assault. In cases of stalking, when the victim and perpetrator had a prior relationship, police and laypeople could not identify the stalking behavior (Weller, Hope, & Sheridan, 2013), reinforcing the myth that stalking was a crime between strangers. Flowers from a stalker are not a "nice thing" to do. When a client of mine found her routinely bought Starbucks coffee sitting on her car one morning as she tried to escape her ex-boyfriend, she got the response of "isn't that sweet" or "at least he isn't mad at you." No one was able to see the implications of that behavior—that he was following her, knew her routine, and was surreptitiously violating the Protection from Abuse order.

The idea that "real" rape includes physical violence, injury, and active resistance persists as well. Despite decades of education about sexual assault, there is continued public acceptance of rape myths (Grubb & Turner, 2012). The belief that sexual assault produces injury lives on, even in spite of consistent evidence that most sexual assault does not produce physical or genital injuries (Truman & Morgan, 2014). Acquittal rates of sexual assault increase when the defendant's arguments highlight the lack of injury or lack of force, even in child sexual-assault cases (Stolzenberg & Lyon, 2014), even though medical literature consistently indicates that lack of injury is the norm, even in cases of penetrative offenses (Adams, Harper, Knudson, & Revilla, 1994). As McDonald (2009) notes, "the less a sexual assault looks like 'real' rape—because a complainant was previously in a relationship with the defendant, had been drinking, or willingly went home with the defendant—the more likely the defendant will be acquitted" (Temkin and Krahe, cited in McDonald, 2009).

Rape myth acceptance is a measurable phenomenon and has been researched since the 1970s (see Grubb & Turner, 2012 for a review). Accepting myths and misinformation about rape has been directly correlated with increased propensity for violence against women in abusers, generally misogynistic intolerance, a distorted perception about the abundance of false allegations of rape, and victim blaming (Flood & Pease, 2009; Hockett, Saucier, Hoffman, Smith, & Craig, 2009). Because rape myths generally include skepticism about claims of rape, mitigation of perpetrator responsibility, and maximization of victim culpability for rape, it is directly related to victim blaming and acquittal in court.

The problem of myth acceptance and victim blaming is pervasive with most kinds of interpersonal violence. For intimate partner violence (IPV), surveys continue to demonstrate that men blame victims for being victims, a finding that is magnified when the victim is a man (Sylaska & Walters, 2014). In one study, acceptance of myths about domestic violence contributed significantly to victim blaming and minimization of the offenses, especially when the victim returned to the offender (Yamawaki, Ochoa-Shipp, Pulsipher, Harlos, & Swindler, 2012). Again, men blamed victims more than women did in this study.

The public's (and victims') continued misperception of and misinformation about violence impacts so many levels of the criminal justice system—reporting violence, cooperation through the investigation and prosecution, investigation of claims by law enforcement, juror decision-making, defense arguments, and retaliation against the victim. When the victim does not label the violence accurately, blames herself, or does not feel believed or supported by the community, the likelihood that the victim will pursue prosecution lessens significantly. "What's the point? No one will believe me anyway." "My mother will kill me—she told me this would happen." "It's my fault anyway. I shouldn't have provoked him." "Those cops were assholes—I knew they didn't believe me. They kept asking me the same things over and over." "It's not like he really hurt me. I mean, it's not like he really raped me, he just wouldn't stop, that's all." "He didn't punch me or anything—he's not that bad." These are all things I have heard victims say. The good news is that a positive experience with the system increases the likelihood that victims of intimate partner violence will seek help from the system again (Cattaneo & Goodman, 2010). Procedural justice and a positive experience with the system also can increase long-term well-being and the mental health of the victims of intimate partner violence, even if a victim initially returns to their abuser (Calton & Cattaneo, 2014).

Interestingly, the public's reliance on "common sense" about intimate violence is skewed so that offenders are supported and victims are blamed or disbelieved. One of the most prevalent and persistent myths is the belief that women lie about being raped (Ben-David & Schneider, 2005, cited in Grubb & Turner, 2012). Time and time again, I encounter groups in public or in law enforcement who cite that 50% of claims of abuse are false, even though the research (again) consistently demonstrates that fabricated allegations are by far the minority of claims of abuse—between 2–8% (Lonsway, Archambault, & Lisak, 2009)! Not only do these ideas go against science, they go against common sense. For example, when we look at delayed disclosure, people expect victims to tell immediately. Yet, if something embarrassing, shameful, or humiliating happens to us—like being yelled at by the boss for a mistake—most of us do not want to discuss it immediately, never mind have the situation scrutinized publicly! We hardly discuss marital problems with strangers, but we expect victims to reveal that their spouses are violent and that they have stayed with that person.

Just as jurors and community members maintain myths about violence and offenders, the victims themselves do this also. The victim's internalized belief system about rape, abuse, or violence can dramatically influence that victim's response during and after the offense. The more a victim believes the myths about rape or victim response, the less likely the victim is to identify him- or herself as having been assaulted, to report the assault, or to cooperate with prosecution. The internalized "scripts" about rape, sexual assault, and domestic violence impact the victim's behavior in the face of abuse throughout the entire process of abuse and prosecution.

When Rape Meets the Myth

Despite information to the contrary, many still adhere to mythical stereotypes of "real" rape. These assaults include a stranger, injury, violence, and surprise attacks. In studies that examine victim behavior in these types of attacks, there are some differences in victim response during and following the assault. There is, in general, a greater likelihood that the victim will report the assault to officials, struggle more physically, show more injury, and experience less blame than victims of assaults by known offenders. However, even the most recent studies show that physically violent resistance, screaming, or attempts to flee were the behaviors of the minority of victims (Woodhams, Hollin, Bull, & Cooke, 2011; Hauffe & Porter, 2009). What might be more important is that there is a greater chance that the victim will be believed and supported by the community when attacked by a stranger if, of course, there is nothing she can be blamed for that would be considered as "inviting" the assault. Even when juries are presented with cases in which the victim was injured, jury members can construct explanations for the injuries (e.g., "rough sex") if the jury believes that the offender knew the victim or if the injuries did not "prove" that the victim struggled vigorously enough to prevent the attack (Ellison & Munro, 2013).

What Are the Facts?

Most of the facts regarding sexual assault are highlighted above. Most victims are assaulted by people they know. Most sexual assault does not cause injury. Most victims do not report immediately, if at all. Even stranger assaults go unreported half of the time. Weapons are used in a minority of reported assaults. Of the thousands of convicted offenders I have interviewed or evaluated, only a small portion used a weapon or were physically violent in their sexual assaults. Even those that committed intimate partner violence or child abuse used physical violence far less than the stereotype would suggest. They rely upon control through fear, anticipation, and terror of violence after they have established their propensity for it with the victims.

The other facts are that victims continue to be blamed. They continue to be disbelieved, even if the perpetrator has other allegations. Recent times have revealed many high-profile cases of public figures who admitted to committing sexual assault or to engaging in coercive or nonconsensual sexual behavior. Despite this, victim allegations were treated with suspicion. Victims were accused of being "gold diggers," attention seekers, and liars. Defense arguments in cases of violence and assault continue to utilize the public's reliance on and acceptance of myths about sexual assault and interpersonal violence to win acquittals, evoking the terms "he said, she said" or highlighting the situations that trigger disclosure in adults and children, like divorce, custody, removal from the offender, and the disclosure of other victims. Finally, it is necessary and useful to combat misinformation about interpersonal violence in the courtroom to increase the chance of successful prosecution.

Why Do I Need to Know This?

Anyone interested in the successful investigation and prosecution of interpersonal violence has a responsibility to understand and communicate the reality and context of the victim and his or her choices. As an investigator, prosecutor, advocate, or other helper, you will encounter victim behaviors, choices, and reactions that are puzzling, confusing, or challenging. You will face your own doubts and struggles in working with assault victims, as the interpersonal impact of violence is profound.

Understanding and addressing problematic expectations and acceptance of myths about sexual assault and violence during the prosecutorial process will allow effective confrontation issues in case to increase chances of a successful prosecution. The key to success is offender focuses prosecution. Simply put, these issues must be framed as "why did he do that" (the assault), *not* "why did she react this way!" These internalized, misinformed beliefs about violence and sexual assault present barriers to investigation and prosecution in many layers of the process, including:

- Inhibiting or precluding victim cooperation and honesty;
- Creating jury bias and impacting jury selection;
- Contributing to effective defense arguments that rely upon myth acceptance; and
- Sentencing that does not reflect the seriousness of the offender's behavior and fails to hold the offender accountable.

Frankly, a prosecutor who does not know or understand victim behaviors him- or herself is unlikely to be able to address the issues in the case. The prosecutor might face feelings of incompetence or an inability to present the "bad" or challenging facts to a jury. A case may not go forward because of a presumption that the jury will not understand the victim or that an acquittal is inevitable. When successful prosecution is a goal for an office, more complex cases might be left behind. If we can redefine success as exposing the offender, supporting the victim, and educating the judiciary, juries, and panels, then more prosecutors might have the willingness to address sexual assault or domestic violence as we typically see it.

Summary

Victim responses and behaviors are actually highly adaptable and expected behaviors of the victim in the face of an assault, providing that the context of the victim and influence of the offender are understood. In general, people rely on prior experiences and knowledge in knowing how to react to a new situation. We count on what is familiar as a template for our responses. For most, being sexually assaulted or physically abused is unfamiliar. It is disorienting, frightening, confusing, and chaotic. Only prior experience with abuse or assault equips any victim with any possible resource. And that response is not always effective.

Abuse and abusers are as individualistic as victim response. What will placate one abuser could agitate another. A strategy to resist or avoid might be successful in stopping one attacker but would prolong the attack of another. Even the same strategy at different times with the same abuser can have different results. The most difficult characteristic of abuse is its inconsistency and unpredictability. It is critical to remember these things when attempting to understand a victim of violence. Understanding how to thoroughly and knowledgably investigate and interview, as well as prosecute these crimes through understanding the victims and offenders, will increase the chances of successful prosecution.

In conclusion:

- There is no such thing as "counterintuitive victim behavior"—it is our faulty expectations based on misinformation and acceptance of myths about assault.
- There is consistent research that demonstrates the persistence of myth acceptance and its detrimental impact on investigation and prosecution of interpersonal violence.
- Victim response to assault is determined by a complex interaction of internal factors, external factors, and influence of the offender.
- Addressing the misunderstanding about victim behaviors is crucial to facilitate better investigation and prosecution of interpersonal violence. This is important throughout the prosecutorial process.
- Many courts have recognized the complex issue of victim dynamics and allow expert testimony on victim behavior to combat jury/judge/layperson reliance on myths and misinformation to determine assault cases.

References

Adams, J., Harper, K., Knudson, S., & Revilla, J. (1994). Examination findings in legally confirmed child sexual abuse: It's normal to be normal. *Pediatrics, 94,* 310–317.

Calton, J., & Cattaneo, L. B. (2014). The effects of procedural and distributive justice on intimate partner violence victims' mental health and likelihood of future help-seeking. *American Journal of Orthopsychiatry, 84,* 329–340.

Campbell, R. (2012, December 3). The neurobiology of sexual assault. *An NIJ Research for the Real World Seminar.* National Institute of Justice: US Department of Justice. Retrieved from www.nij.gov/multimedia/presenter/presenter-campbell/Pages/welcome.aspx

Cattaneo, L. B., & Goodman, L. A. (2010). Through the lens of therapeutic jurisprudence: The relationship between empowerment in the court system and well-being for intimate partner violence victims. *Journal of Interpersonal Violence, 25,* 482–502.

Davies, M., Gilston, J., & Rogers, P. (2012). Examining the relationships between male rape myth acceptance, female rape myth acceptance, victim blame, homophobia, gender roles, and ambivalent sexism. *Journal of Interpersonal Violence, 27*(14), 2807–2823. doi:10.1177/0886260512438281

Dutton, M. A. (2009). Update of the "Battered Woman Syndrome" critique. *Applied Research Forum.* National Online Resource Center on Violence Against Women. Retrieved from www.vawnet.org

Ellison, L. (2005). Closing the credibility gap: The prosecutorial use of expert witness testimony in sexual assault cases. *The International Journal of Evidence and Proof, 9,* 239–268.

Ellison, L., & Munro, V. (2013). Better the devil you know? 'Real rape' stereotypes and the relevance of a previous relationship in (mock) juror deliberations. *The International Journal of Evidence & Proof, 17,* 299–322. doi:10.1350/ijep.2013.17.4.433

Fanflik, P. (2007). *Victim response to sexual assault: Counterintuitive or simply adaptive?* Washington, DC: National District Attorney's Association.

Federal Bureau of Investigation, National Incident-Based Reporting System, 2012–2014. (2015). Retrieved from https://ucr.fbi.gov/crime-in-the-u.s/2015/crime-in-the-u.s.-2015/offenses-known-to-law-enforcement/national-data

Flood, M., & Pease, B. (2009). Factors influencing attitudes to violence against women. *Trauma Violence Abuse, 10*(2), 125–142. doi:10.1177/1524838009334131

Grubb, A., & Turner, E. (2012). Attribution of blame in rape cases: A review of the impact of rape myth acceptance, gender role conformity and substance use on victim blaming. *Aggression and Violent Behavior, 17*(5), 443–452.

Hauffe, S., & Porter, L. (2009). An interpersonal comparison of lone and group rape offenses. *Psychology, Crime and Law, 15,* 469–491. doi:10.1080/ 106831 60802409339

Hockett, J., Saucier, D., Hoffman, B., Smith, S., & Craig, A. (2009). Oppression through acceptance: Predicting rape myth acceptance and attitudes towards victims. *Violence Against Women, 15*(8), 877–897. doi:10.1177/1077801209335489

Littleton, H., & Breitkopf, C. R. (2006). Coping with the experience of rape. *Psychology of Women Quarterly, 30*, 106–116.

Long, J. (2007). *Introducing expert testimony to explain victim behavior in sexual and domestic violence prosecutions.* Washington, DC: National District Attorney's Association.

Long, J., Kristiansson, V., & Mallios, C. (2013). When and how: Admitting expert testimony on victim behavior in sexual assault cases in Pennsylvania. *Strategies in Brief,* 18.

Lonsway, K., Archambault, J., & Lisak, D. (2009). False reports: Moving beyond the issue to successfully investigate and prosecute non-stranger sexual assault. *The Voice, 3*(1). American Prosecutor's Research Institute.

McDonald, E. (2009). Temkin & Krahe, sexual assault and the justice gap: A question of attitude. *Pace Law Review, 29*(2), 349–376. Retrieved from http://digitalcommons.pace.edu/plr/vol29/iss2/6

Mennicke, A., Anderson, D., Oehme, K., & Kennedy, S. (2014). Law enforcement officers' perception of rape and rape victims: A multimethod study. *Violence and Victims, 29*(5), 815–827.

Paquette, D. (2016, February 2). A new wrinkle in the Cosby saga. *The Washington Post.* Retrieved from www.washingtonpost.com

Planty, M., & Langton, L. (2016). *Special report: Female victims of sexual violence, 1994–2010.* (NCJ Publication 240665). US Department of Justice: Bureau of Justice Statistics. Retrieved from www.bjs.gov/content/pub/pdf/fvsv9410.pdf

Stolzenberg, S., & Lyon, T. (2014). Evidence Summarized in attorney's closing arguments predicts acquittals in criminal trials of child sexual abuse. *Child Maltreatment, 19*(2), 119–129. doi:10.1177/107755951453988

Sylaska, K., & Walters, A. S. (2014). Testing the extent of the gender trap: College students' perceptions of and reactions to intimate partner violence. *Sex Roles,* 70, 134–145.

Truman, J., & Morgan, R. (2014). *Criminal victimization, 2013.* (NCJ Publication 247648). US Department of Justice, BJS Web. Retrieved from www.bjs.gov/content/pub/pdf/cv13.pdf

Truman, J., & Morgan, R. (2016). *Criminal victimization, 2015.* (NCJ Publication 250180). US Department of Justice, BJS Web. Retrieved from www.bjs.gov/content/pub/pdf/cv15.pdf

Weller, M., Hope, L., & Sheridan, L. (2013). Police and public perceptions of stalking: The role of prior victim- offender relationship. *Journal of Interpersonal Violence, 28*(2), 320–339. doi:10.1177/0886260512454718

Woodhams, J., Hollin, C., Bull, R., & Cooke, C. (2011). Behavior displayed by female victims during rapes committed by lone and multiple perpetrators. *Psychology, Public Policy, and Law, 18*(3), 415–452.

Yamawaki, N., Ochoa-Shipp, M., Pulsipher, C., Harlos, A., & Swindler, S. (2012). Perceptions of domestic violence: The effects of domestic violence myths, victim's relationship with her abuser, and the decision to return to her abuser. *Journal of Interpersonal Violence, 27*(16), 3195–3212. doi:10.1177/0886260512441253

Chapter 2

"I Was in Shock"
Internal Factors Impacting Victim Response

> *I was in shock. I just didn't know what to do. I couldn't believe this was happening. What was happening? I froze.*
> —*Adult woman raped by a friend*

Why did she do *that?* Why *didn't* she do that? Of all the factors that influence victim response during and after an assault, the internal factors are likely the most immediately powerful. These factors can be grouped into three areas: emotional; cognitive; and beliefs/values/culture. Each of us carries within us a skill set, a set of beliefs and values, and a set of experiences that guide our responses, choices, understanding of ourselves and others, and our ability to manage and react to challenging situations. Sexual assault and interpersonal violence offer perhaps the most challenging and confusing situations to which to respond. Sexual and intimate violence challenges us at our core; it involves the most primary and intimate experiences we have.

Given that assault is one of the most private experiences we can have, the victim's response to or behavior during or after an assault is influenced by some of the most personal internal factors that the victim carries within him or her. A victim experiencing an assault is immersed in an experience in which feelings and reason struggle against each other and cooperate in order to facilitate survival. Decisions are made intuitively and strategically. Some of these factors are natural cognitive processes that occur in everyone. Others are personal to the individual. Beliefs and values around the victim's identity, understanding of gender and sexuality, skills with negotiation and conflict, cultural and social factors, and even religious tenets all play a role in the victim's perception of, understanding of, and response to violent assault. These internal factors are important to understand to be able to explain what made a victim act the way she or he did.

Fear

During an attack, whether a physical or sexual assault, the brain's primary and immediate response is fear. When threat is identified and when the victim understands that the attack is inevitable, regardless of how the process of that attack occurred, fear is the natural response (Kozlowska, Walker, McLean, & Carrive, 2015). The victim might fear the violation, the act itself, pain, or the perpetrator. She might fear being seen in a vulnerable position or the consequences of the attack. A victim can fear that the attack might be worse if the abuser is provoked. Victims fear getting pregnant or a disease. A myriad of fear-based thoughts can go through a victim's mind during an attack—or no thoughts at all, as terror and fear make the victim freeze.

Emotional Impact of Fear

As an emotion, fear enhances our assessment of the potential for harm and decreases our likelihood of engaging in risky options like fighting back (Baron, 2007). This means fear may cause someone to overestimate the danger of resistance, perceive the abuser as capable of being more violent than he might be, or feel great peril when considering an unfamiliar behavior. So, a victim who is not in the habit of being aggressive and fighting back would be less likely to fight back or scream. To overcome fear and to act in one's own defense require the development of habits for self-defense (Hopper, 2018), which most victims are unlikely to have. If the victim has a prior history of abuse, she might rely on old habits, like submission, dissociation, or pacification of the offender, that have worked in the past.

Fear not only influences the victim's decision during an assault, but after it as well. Fear pervades decision-making throughout the victim's experience. The victim might fear retaliation by the perpetrator or others. He might fear that no one will believe him. She can fear the consequences of disclosure or of antagonizing the abuser by avoiding him. There can be many possible sources of fear for the victim, all of which should be explored and acknowledged as affecting the victim's thinking and behavior. The fear of consequences for telling and not being believed might arise immediately, sometimes overshadowing the impact of the assault.

Physiological Impact of Fear

Fear has a profound physiological impact. We have evolved to defend ourselves. In the time of threat, we are hardwired to respond. Physiological

20 Victim Response to Interpersonal Violence

responses to threat are complex and often out of our control. When faced with a serious threat, a series of responses occurs. This is referred to as the "defense cascade" (Kozlowska et al., 2015). Many responses are active, like flight or fight, but some are passive, like freezing or tonic immobility. Freezing is generally an immediate but transient response. People experience an array of physiological changes that ready the body for the attack. Prior trauma or adverse experiences can "prime" someone to experience freezing (Kozlowska et al., 2015). A victim who freezes might experience more terror or decide while frozen to submit to the assault. "I was literally frozen," the victim explained when she awoke to find the perpetrator penetrating her from behind. "I tried to open my mouth to scream and nothing came out. I have never felt anything like that before. Then it was too late anyway."

A victim who freezes during an attack can get stuck there in a response known as "tonic immobility." Tonic immobility is a very primal defense mechanism, basically "playing dead" when faced by a threat to confuse or discourage the attacker. In humans, it is elicited in situations when escape or fighting is impossible (Kozlowska et al., 2015). In the sexual assault literature, it sometimes is referred to as "rape paralysis." Although freezing is brief, tonic immobility can last for substantially longer. Research demonstrates that there is evidence to support the existence of tonic immobility in humans (Volchan et al., 2011). And sexual assault is one the most likely events that trigger tonic immobility. Not only that, but both male and female victims who experience tonic immobility are more likely to have post-traumatic symptoms (Coxwell & King, 2010). It is critical to understand this phenomenon, as recent studies show that most victims of sexual assault experience some level of feeling paralyzed (Russo, 2017).

Finally, the experience of intense fear or terror can leave victims exhausted. There is an adrenal dump in self-protection and recuperation. Exhaustion can set in and cause severe lethargy. Decision-making can be compromised. The victim might literally be unable to consider escape or leaving. Referred to as quiescent immobility, it is the state of complete exhaustion that occurs after a trauma when the victim has returned to a state of relative safety, like when an attack is over (Kozlowska et al., 2015). Although adaptive for healing, it is maladaptive for the expectations we place on victims.

Cognitive Biases and Unexpected Decisions

Predictably Irrational (Ariely, 2008) is a fascinating book that analyzes and exposes "hidden forces" that impact decision-making. Ariely (2008) describes these factors that affect spending, loving, choosing, sex, thinking, and trusting. Some of those factors that cause problems in our ability to make predictable or "logical" decisions are cognitive biases. Cognitive biases are predispositions in thinking that guide or push our decision-making. Decades of research have supported the findings that all of us hold these biases, that they are highly consistent, and that they can in fact predict decision-making (Hilbert, 2012). There are many of these biases, some very well researched. In fact, a long list of biases and related research can be found easily on the internet and are described more thoroughly in books like *Thinking and Deciding* (Baron, 2007). Some of the most relevant ones include loss aversion, confirmation bias, familiarity and perception of risk, personal control, habituation, and personalization of risk. These biases not only impact the victim but affect the jury as well.

Loss Aversion

In this author's experience, cognitive bias is not typically examined as an element in victim decision-making, both during and after the offense. Although there are many types of biases, there are several that I believe can be directly linked to understanding many things relevant to understanding victim and offender behavior. For instance, loss aversion describes the intense reluctance we as humans have for losing something, creating a pressure that could be twice as powerful as our need to gain something (Kahneman, 2011). We will spend money needlessly to avoid losing a bargain, something marketers rely on! We experience pain more vividly than we experience joy—loss is one of the most painful things of all (Brafman & Brafman, 2011).

This is a potent bias that impacts decisions in relationships as well. Consider the importance of a relationship, perhaps one of the most important things to most people. Loss aversion increases the more meaningful a loss becomes (Brafman & Brafman, 2011). Imagine choosing to lose a lover, marriage, history, or partner. A victim's decision to return to an offender can be about avoiding loss, rather than gaining freedom from abuse. Leaving an abuser can mean loss of a family, a home, dreams, hopes, and investment of time and love. It can include loss of extended family or friends, commitment to religious promises, esteem and value, and many other major or subtle things. Even believing that someone you trusted can betray you by hurting you or your child includes significant losses. "I loved him. We planned to be together. Even if I was still only going to be his side girl, I was okay with that," said one woman who was raped and beaten by her lover. She went on, "I mean, we had so much history together—so many memories! Who could I call about something stupid we thought was funny together? Even after everything, I still miss that stuff."

Confirmation Bias: "See, I Told You He Wasn't Like That"

There are other things at play as well, like confirmation bias. This bias ensures that once the belief is in place and we are invested in it, we collect information in a biased way to confirm that belief (Kahneman, 2011). We can apply this cognitive process to victims of violence. Confirmation bias impacts the victim's beliefs and decision-making on many levels.

In the identification of abuse itself, if the victim holds a specific definition of abuse, rape, or assault, the victim will look for evidence to confirm or deny what has happened to her. As we discussed in the internalization of rape script, when a rape does not conform to internalized definitions of rape, the victim has difficulty identifying the rape. A victim does not find evidence to "confirm" she was raped—unless, of course, there is other information, perhaps from someone else, that can reinforce the victim's sense of harm, feelings of betrayal, or experience of trauma. "I knew something happened, I knew something was wrong," one victim stated during her testimony. "But it wasn't until I talked to my friend. She said, 'You was raped.'"

The same is true for the victim's understanding of the offender. Remember, to identify yourself as abused, you have to identify the person who harmed you as an abuser. If the victim believes that "down deep" the offender is good, kind, loving, misunderstood, or is not capable of being a rapist, the victim will look for evidence to confirm that belief. (Not only the victim does this—it is a common defense tactic and is used by the offender's community to disbelieve the victim.) This is complicated by the fact that the victim has invested in the abuser. She loves and has dreams with him and has hope for them together. The victim has experiences with the offender that may be joyful, comforting, and loving. Confirmation bias will be used by the victim to "prove" her belief in the offender's goodness or innocence to maintain her attachment to him.

The mistake many helpers make with victims is to try to disprove the victim's belief about the offender, as opposed to adding more information to that belief. A victim can mightily resist a helper, family member, or prosecutor who tries to tell her that she is in love with a bad person. She will have an armament of evidence to disprove that. In fact, an element of successful intervention (and prosecution) is to exploit confirmation bias! By adding information and examples about what abuse is, in an educative way, you can create a new belief that can be confirmed. "I really didn't understand that what he was doing was abuse! I mean, it felt wrong, it hurt, but when I heard him say the exact things you had taught me about, I thought, 'There it is,'" victims will say to me. Another clinician of mine was just told by a victim who stayed with the person who abused her and her children, "you told me that a lot of these guys say that. You told me, then, bam, there he was saying the same shit. I thought,

'I heard this already.'" A victim, prosecutor, or expert can do the same for your juries and panels.

Offenders will use confirmation bias as well, manipulating it with people to "prove" their innocence. "You know me! I am not that type of person," he will insist. The offender might bring in others that he has not beaten or raped to show that he is not capable of the assault. "He doesn't treat me that way" or "I have never seen him like that" is something people will say about offenders to support their beliefs about him. Offenders' use of this bias will be discussed further in a later chapter.

Familiarity and Perception of Risk

There are also cognitive issues in the perception of risk. It is well-established that we underestimate risk of familiar things, like driving to work, and overestimate the risk of unusual things or things we have not experienced (Gardner, 2009). This is well-described in Daniel Gardner's book *The Science of Fear*. He describes throughout how humans become extraordinarily fearful of unlikely things, like a terrorist attack, but accept and underestimate the risk of driving to work each day.

Apply this understanding to victims. In intimate partner violence or child abuse, victims live day to day with their abusers. They are familiar with the abusers' habits, moods, and reactions. Despite the unpredictability and inconsistency of abuse, victims are accustomed to the abuser. They can establish a perhaps false sense of control and influence over their abuse and, because of their experience, underestimate risk. After all, they have survived the abuse, maybe reuniting afterwards in a highly rewarding way. After the terror has passed, the victim feels gratitude and relief, giving the abuser "credit" for being kind again. "I would listen and know the minute he came in the door what kind of night it would be," the wife explained to me. The simple way he shut the door would tell her if she was in for conflict, possibly an assault. "I was so relieved when it was fine. But even when it wasn't, it would be bad for awhile," she went on to explain. "But then the storm would pass and it would be over. We sometimes could have a nice night after that."

Attempting to instill, or have the victim acknowledge even a reasonable level of, fear for the abuser is difficult. It is terrifying for helpers and attorneys to see the signs of lethality in the abuse of the victim while the victim doesn't. However, remember: the abuse is only a portion of the relationship with the offender. The rest of the relationship might not be dangerous or might be reinforcing to the victim. Of course, this can change over time with abusers. They can escalate, which is something that can trigger reporting in the victim. Or an effective helper can educate the victim about the real level of risk involved.

This faulty perception of risk can impact post-offense behaviors as well. After being raped or assaulted, a victim might fall asleep in bed with the perpetrator, go to breakfast with him, or finish watching the movie. Sometimes this is a result of exhaustion. Sometimes it is fear of provoking the offender. Sometimes it is simply a misguided assessment of risk. "I mean, I just wanted it to be over. I thought I could just wait for him to go to sleep and leave me alone," one woman said, trying to explain why she did not struggle during a rape after being strangled or did not escape when the offender fell asleep. Even though her assailant had never assaulted or raped her before, she felt safe because she was familiar with his behavior after they had sex. He would usually go to sleep in a positive mood. She assessed the rape as the same experience. Unfortunately, when he woke up, he slapped her and raped her again.

Fear encompasses more than fear of danger. Remember, fear and perceived risk of the familiar is less than fear and perceived risk of the unfamiliar. A victim who has been involved with an abuser might fear the unfamiliarity of being alone. When combined with the impact of being abused, devalued, and degraded, being alone can feel very risky for the victim. This may be unreasonable, produced by the offender's brainwashing of the victim that she is not lovable or desirable. Or, the assessment of risk could be very accurate, like the victim's fear of leaving the perpetrator. Many homicides of abuse victims occur when they leave the perpetrator.

Personal Control, Fear, and Risk

The idea of personal control is also a factor in fear and understanding risk. When we believe things are beyond our control, we are more fearful (Gardner, 2009). Again, apply this to victim response and thinking. If the victim is experiencing the offender or the assault as beyond his or her control, it is terrifying. Regarding rape, this is the element of the "rape script" that is most fear-inducing. Being attacked by a stranger in an unexpected way with a weapon or violence is the most frightening narrative of rape. However, if the victim has been drinking, accepted a ride, was provocative during an argument, "broke the rules," or "got herself in that situation," then the assault is less frightening. The victim can feel that she had control of elements of the assault, so can believe she can or should have made different. "If I only hadn't . . ." begins many victims' litany of "bad choices" she imagines would have prevented the abuse. This is not only true for the victim—it is true for the audience as well. Almost all victim blaming adds an element of victim control that mitigates the terrifying nature of assault. Again the offender exploits this, convincing the victim she had control. "If you hadn't pushed my buttons" is a great example of this.

Gardner (2009) also speaks of the factor of "voluntariness" in the assessment of risk and experience of fear. If we have chosen to engage in the risk, we are less afraid. If we haven't "volunteered" for the risk, it is much more frightening. Again, apply this concept to an attack by a stranger. This is why this narrative of assault is so seductive and terrifying. No one volunteered for it. But, for example, a woman who goes out drinking and goes home with a strange man "volunteered" for her risk. Subsequently, she is much more likely to be blamed (Grubb & Turner, 2012), not only by others, but also blamed internally by herself. I mean, "what did she expect," making choices like that?

As humans, we avoid the experience of fear. We engage in all types of ways to cope with our fear. But, in truth, what is more frightening to anyone than to be abused or assaulted by someone they love? What is more terrifying than to trust someone else with all the good judgment we have, only to be betrayed and harmed? If we acknowledge the arbitrary, unpredictable, and invisible threat of someone we know, love, and trust being an abuser or rapist, what do we have left?

Habituation

Habituation to fear is another cognitive process that needs to be acknowledged in understanding victim dynamics, especially in victims who endure ongoing abuse by their perpetrators. We become used to stressors (Gardner, 2009). This is especially important in understanding coping with risk and fear. We cannot live in a constant state of arousal and fear, so we habituate to these experiences. "I thought it was normal, the way he talked to me. I mean, at first it bothered me, but over time, I thought this was just the way it was," a client recently told me. She then produced an audiotape of her husband after he got irritated with the mistake she presumably made. "Jesus Christ, you stupid fucking bitch! Don't you ever think! Christ, guess I just have to do everything myself—useless," he said to her in a contemptuous tone. This was just a part of the excerpt. It was only when she taped how he spoke to her and listened to it through another person's ears that she could identify how verbally abusive he was on an ongoing basis. Why? Habituation.

There are many, many cognitive processes that we all experience on a daily basis, simply as part of the human experience. However, we forget about them when it comes to understanding victim behavior and, perhaps even more importantly, our response to understanding assault and abusers.

Personalization of Risk

Another element that affects an assessment of risk and fear is the appraisal of how personal a risk is. We tend to evaluate risk and danger on a very personal level: if it is dangerous to me, it is riskier and more frightening (Gardner, 2009). Again, let's apply this to abuse and assault: strangers,

26 Victim Response to Interpersonal Violence

whether they are rapists or pedophiles, can pose a danger to me. They are unknown and unpredictable. However, the abuser who is a friend or is known to the victim is perceived as less of risk. The victim might accommodate to an experienced assault ("the devil you know"), minimizing it, while fearing a more "serious" danger ("the devil you don't").

This occurs generally, too, with helpers or others assessing the dangerousness of an offender. If the offender is familiar to the audience or only abuses within his family, he is not likely to be perceived as a personalized risk. If the victim can be blamed for "bad" decisions, the risk is not personalized to others. When people who know the offender say to themselves, "well, he was never that way to me/my kids," they are using this bias to cloud their assessment of the offender, perhaps overtly or covertly blaming the victim in the process ("she must push his buttons"). Sometimes I hear the acronym NIMBY (Not in My Back Yard) to describe this. If an offender is dangerous to me or mine, get rid of him. If he only hurts his own kids, it is only a family problem, not a community problem. In fact, an effective prosecution tool is to key in on questions that would personalize the experience, like asking jurors about their daughter that goes to college when prosecuting a college rape. The personalization of the danger of the offender tends to increase the audience's assessment of the risk of that offender.

These are only a few of the cognitive biases that can impact victim behaviors. The victim might not even be aware that they exist. However, a knowledgeable investigator, interviewer, or prosecutor can expose these biases and explain them, making them familiar to the judge or jury.

Culture and Religion

> I was told my whole life that I was short and Asian, so I was target and I needed to be careful.
> —*Victim describing her "education" about rape*

Each victim comes from a particular culture, subculture, or both. The culture can be understood as the complex constellation of beliefs, values, morals, social rules, and customs. The culture could be a racial culture, the culture of the community, a family culture, or religious culture. There are many subcultures that impact victim response; for example, the subculture of the military or the college environment. Within a culture context, there are values and beliefs about men, women, sex, gender roles, family, community, and assault that strongly influence a victim's response to assault. These cultures can have a profound effect on the individual's decision-making and perception regarding domestic violence, sexual assault, drinking, and sexuality.

Culture: "That's Normal for Them; It's a Cultural Thing"

Some cultures maintain particular beliefs and values about gender roles and rape itself. For example, in one case in which I was involved, the victim was a Vietnamese woman. She explained that in her culture, rape destroyed a woman, permanently eradicating her desirability. "No one wants to eat from a dirty bowl," she stated, as a way to explain how violated women are perceived in her worldview. Because of this, her response to her rapist was to try to maintain her desirability to him. He had professed to like her and find her attractive. He held a job of status in her culture. After he initially raped her, he continued to her pursue her, texting and calling. Eventually, he persuaded her to send him topless photos with the promise of an ongoing relationship. Because she believed that no one else could or would ever love her, she began to consider the man a boyfriend. After the third rape, she could no longer maintain her interest in him. She did not come forward until the perpetrator's other victims had come forward. In fact, she was found by investigators and reported the rapes. Throughout, she was a reluctant witness whose family never learned that she was involved in a rape prosecution.

There are similar issues in some Middle Eastern cultures. In India, reporting of sexual assault is rare and justice for victims is "elusive." In an interview on the podcast Breakdown (Edwards, 2017), Dr. Paramita Chattoraj, a law professor at KIIT University in India, stated that there is a "staunch and very strong stigma attached to rape and sexual offenses." In the culture, she explained, "there is an inherent idea of dignity or modesty of a woman which is almost sacred to a woman." Regarding sexual assault, she said, "if any man tries to fondle with that dignity or modesty, it is not just the woman who is disgraced, but the whole family is disgraced, which has an implication on marriage prospects of other girls of the family, because girl's marriage is a big thing in India." Obviously, these types of cultural issues impact disclosure, prosecution, protection, and intervention in sexual assault and with sexual offenders. Research demonstrates the persistence of the impact of Mexican American culture on victims' identification, disclosure, and reporting of intimate partner violence. The cultural values of machismo, family, women's roles, and inevitability of harm directly affect a victim and her community. The culture also influences the victims' decision to stay (Valdovinos & Mechanic, 2017) and the development of post-traumatic symptoms (Cuevas, Sabina, & Picard, 2015).

The culture of the victim can influence jury perception as well. If the culture or subculture is perceived in a pejorative or distorted way, domestic violence or sexual assault may be minimized or accepted by outsiders. For example, in cases involving college students, juries may perceive "drunk sex" or "hookups" to be so common that they dismiss the seriousness of an alcohol-facilitated sexual assault. A defense attorney once confronted me during my testimony about an assault at a fraternity house about my familiarity with "hookup" culture and whether or not I understood "one-night stands." The defense attorney went so far as to suggest that being grabbed by the back of the head and shoved towards the man's crotch was the "universal sign for a blow job" among college students. In fact, the offender was forcing the victim's head onto his penis. The perpetrator was convicted of sexually assaulting the young woman, who had not consented.

If the subculture or culture is perceived as violent, or if the jury relies on negative stereotypes, the victim may not be well protected. For example, if the jury holds the belief that all Native Americans are violent and alcoholic, the victims of domestic violence who attempt to get intervention might be unsuccessful. If that victim also has internalized negative beliefs about the culture, the victim may tolerate the abuse, accommodate to it, or protect the offender. In my work with certain victims, one victim expressed fear of reporting domestic violence because the reporting would validate racist beliefs about the victim's culture, contributing to her sense of shame. "That's just part of their culture," I have heard. This sentiment was expressed publicly regarding an NFL player's physical abuse of his child; basically, the idea that African American families whip their children as a norm. Juries may hold prejudiced beliefs of "those people" in a variety of contexts that contribute to minimizing, excusing, or ignoring sexual assault or violence in those populations. Flood and Pease (2009) describe the interplay of culture and gender expectations or roles as highly dynamic. These issues are applicable in an array of contexts, like expecting a soldier to "fight back" because he has been trained to fight—forgetting that soldiers are taught to fight in a particular context, not while being raped.

Religion: "But God Says . . ."

> We don't answer to the laws of man, only the laws of God.
> —Sex-offending priest

Religion or religious beliefs can significantly impact a victim's behavior. This may occur at multiple levels for the victim. If the victim is part of a religious society that encourages members to resolve problems in the community by using elders or the church, the victim may not feel supported to get outside help or may not have access to outside services. An example of this might be a community that segregates itself in matters of help-seeking, like the Amish in some areas. The community may home-school children, limiting access to reporting. The religious community may have strong tenets about gender roles, sexuality, or marriage. The victim might struggle with shame or judgment from the community, pressure to comply with community rules, or resistance to going against her lifelong learning.

The issue of marriage can be paramount in some religious communities. The victim's support system might include individuals that prioritize marriage over individual satisfaction or believe in familial hierarchy that dictates the male role of dominance in the family. "I felt pressured to drop the Protection From Abuse order (PFA)," one victim of domestic violence explained. "He [the perpetrator] brought the priest from our church to the house. He promised that [my husband] would never hurt me again."

These situations could impact a victim's help-seeking behavior, decision to return to the relationship, or recantation of abuse allegations. They may also contribute to the victim's sense of shame and culpability for the abuse. Many victims I've treated have been told by church leaders that their job was to be obedient in the marriage and that they were responsible for conflict, even if it entailed abuse.

There are many cultural and religious rules that dictate sexuality. A woman's sexual behavior is frequently scrutinized through this lens, the victim's own scrutiny often being the harshest. If the victim was sexually or physically assaulted in a homosexual relationship, religion might play a role in the protection or secrecy of the relationship, as well as the victim's help-seeking behavior.

Religious and spiritual beliefs can also extensively impact the victim's perception of the offender. If the victim believes in forgiveness, redemption, or that justice comes from God, that victim can be influenced significantly by those beliefs, especially in the prosecutorial process. If the victim hears the offender's regret or professed remorse, the victim may feel that it is her duty to forgive in order to be, for example, a "good Christian" herself. The needs of the criminal justice system can place the victim in direct conflict with her identity as a good person, a good Christian, or a good community member.

It is important to ask victims about the cultural and religious influences on their decision-making involving their victimization. It is important to assess their social supports and community's ability to respond protectively to them. Even a cursory assessment of these issues for the victim might reveal untapped resources or supports in the community that will foster resilience and increase the willingness to participate in the prosecutorial process, while enabling investigators to understand some of the barriers that may be preventing a victim's cooperation.

Beliefs and Values

All of us hold a set of beliefs and values regarding ourselves, others, violence, sexuality, and assault. These beliefs and values infuse how the world looks at us and how we make our decisions. These beliefs and values are both personal, like ideas of personal responsibility, and reflect more general societal views, like acceptance of rape myths.

It's a "Just World" or What Goes Around, Comes Around

There exists, socially, the idea that the world is a "just world" and that what happens to us is inherently linked to our behaviors and what we "deserve." The idea that "things happen for a reason," "what comes around goes around," "karma," and "you brought this on yourself" all reflect the idea that the world responds to you in a fair way. The idea of a "just world," coined by social scientists in the 1960s, is easily identifiable in day-to-day life and even reflected on bumper stickers. Its study was inspired after Lerner and Simmons (1966) watched observers blame the victims of electric shock for their own punishment. Observers "rejected and devalued" victims, blaming them for their own pain in the laboratory. "It seems obvious," the authors wrote, "that most people cannot afford, for the sake of their sanity, to believe in a world governed by a schedule of random reinforcements" (p. 203). Additionally, this study showed that observers blamed and rejected the victim more if there was continued suffering of the victim and the observers were helpless to change the suffering. Imagine how this study applies to the problem of domestic violence, when the victim does not leave the abuser and law enforcement cannot intervene.

There have been many subsequent studies and observations that confirm that observers blame victims for their own abuse, including rape (Grubb & Turner, 2012). More importantly, victims themselves might hold this world view. This idea or belief system is thought to contribute to a victim's feeling of blame and culpability for being sexually assaulted, as well as contributing to society's blaming of the victim. Although victim blaming is easy to identify externally—"what did she think would happen" or "if she hadn't been drinking"—it is more difficult to identify the beliefs that the victim has about his or her own culpability. Victims often will try to make sense of what has happened to them by blaming themselves. Self-blame reflects the idea of a just world and also gives victims a sense of control, especially in an ongoing situation of violence, like domestic violence. Victims will tell themselves, "if I hadn't provoked him," "why did I wear that," "if I only kept my mouth shut," "I should've stayed with my friends," or a myriad of other self-blaming statements. All of these are attempts to understand and manage the confusing and unmanageable experience of assault.

These beliefs of culpability are seductive. They are hard to argue with because they have some truth to them. Most self-blame identifies an undeniable aspect of the offense. If she hadn't gone home alone with the perpetrator, she wouldn't have been raped. If he hadn't broken the rules, his mother wouldn't have beaten him. That sounds like truth and focuses on the victim's choices. However, the victim did not make the choices with the knowledge that she would be assaulted. This type of thinking does not account for the deviance of the offender. Therefore, it relies on faulty logic and hindsight. Certainly no one would have made the same choices if they knew there was going to be an attack or a terrible outcome. This type of thinking relies on the assumption that the decision "deserves" the outcome. I once was arguing with a man about the sexual assault of a victim by a well-known athlete. "What did she think was going to happen," he said with certainty. "I mean, she was underage! She snuck into a bar!" I pointed out that she probably thought she would be grounded if she got caught, not sexually assaulted.

Rape Myth Acceptance and Rape Scripts

Victims have internalized beliefs, including acceptance of rape myths and internalized "rape scripts," that contribute to the victim's assessment of his or her blame for what has happened to them. The victim's definition of assault or idea of how it happens impacts a victim's response on multiple levels, from identifying the perpetrator's intention to harm to choosing whether to participate in prosecution.

Rape myth acceptance is a powerful set of beliefs that has been shown to influence victim behavior, reporting, and cooperating with prosecution of assault (Grubb & Turner, 2012). Rape scripts are those internalized narratives of what rape is, who does it, and how it happens. If a victim believes that rape is a physically violent event by a stranger, then being raped by a known assailant, being coerced, being uninjured, or showing a failure to vigorously resist might prevent a victim from identifying herself as raped or assaulted at all (Turchik, Probst, Irvin, Chau, & Gidycz, 2009), never mind reporting the assault to authorities. Adherence to these beliefs contributes to greater self-blame, shame, and uncertainty about the assault and the offender. In fact, Turchik et al. (2009) found that having a stereotypical rape script actually put victims more at risk of being assaulted in the future.

Victims hold other beliefs and values as well. Some are gender-based, like how men and women need to act sexually or in relationships. For women, being conditioned to be "nice" and to be peacemakers contributes to failure to resist, report, or even understand themselves as abused. Some victims believe that violence is a result of making someone angry and that their abuser has "anger management" problems, not problems with abusing. Victims might believe it is a woman or child's responsibility to manage male sexuality: that if a man gets aroused, rape is a consequence. Victims carry beliefs about themselves—their own worth, power, capability, and lovability. They have beliefs about social supports, independence, and vulnerability, labeling victimization as a result of being "weak." Victims carry beliefs about law enforcement, justice, or retribution. A good investigator or prosecutor will attempt to understand what the victim's values are and how these values impact the victim's choices. An exploration of the victim's beliefs might allow the prosecutor an opportunity to change them, especially if they involve support, justice, or the system.

Confusion About or Failure to Identify the Assault or Abuse

> *I mean, I know it was bad, okay, he had a bad temper. But I didn't know it was abuse. I look at it now and think, 'wow, how could I be so stupid?' But it wasn't until I started to research it that I found out it was abuse.*
>
> —College-educated victim of intimate partner violence

Initially, it seems like abuse would be easy to identify, especially if you are on the receiving end. It is commonly assumed that a victim will be able to identify abuse easily and will take measures to defend, escape, or protect him- or herself. That is false. Research has found repeatedly that a majority of women rape victims fail to label their experience as rape, particularly when a they had a relationship with the offender (Littleton, Axsom, Breitkopf, & Berenson, 2006; Peterson & Muehlenhard, 2011). A meta-analysis of more than 5,900 victims revealed that more than 60% of rape victims failed to identify themselves as having been raped (Wilson & Miller, 2016). Victims often label their experience with offenders as something other than assault or abuse, whether it is sexual, physical, or verbal violence, calling it "bad sex" or "miscommunication" (Wilson & Miller, 2016). "You hurt me during sex. A lot. You didn't care, you didn't care that I said I didn't want it anymore. You just kept going," a victim texted the offender who had raped and strangled her. He responded, "I know what I did was a mistake." He continued, "you never told me I was hurting you." In this case, both the victim and the perpetrator avoided using any word to characterize the assault, coming to the term "sexually and physically harmed" to text about the rape and strangulation.

Often victims do not identify what is happening to them, because of internalized rape myths as well as the generally confusing, disorienting experience of sexual assault. Marital rape can be especially confusing for victims, who may believe that they have no right to refuse the spouse or that prior consenting sexual activity negates the ability for the partner to rape. "I was hysterical crying. I called my mom and told her what happened, he raped me," the victim said. She went on, "she said a man can't rape his wife, you're not giving him enough. I was like, well, that's just what he do then." She had been repeatedly raped by her husband. She added, "I guess the man has to tussle with me for sex." When asked why she stayed with him, the victim said, "I still in my heart didn't want to believe that he did it." The victim in a relationship with a perpetrator is more likely to understand the sexual assault as something going wrong in a sexual situation, rather than as an attack (Phillips, 2000 cited in Littleton et al., 2006).

There are many reasons for a victim's unwillingness or inability to identify the abuse or assault she or he is experiencing. As noted above, the victim might have ideas about what "real" rape is or "real" abuse. If the abuse is more like their view or definition, victims are better able to identify the abuse. Sexual assault is more easily identified by victims who were not involved sexually with the perpetrator, when there was physical force, or when they resisted physically (Kahn, Jackson, Kully, Badger, & Halvorsen, 2003). Victims might not be able to identify the assault because of confusion or shock. Some victims do not label their experiences to avoid the emotional, psychological, or interpersonal ramifications. Many factors impact a victim's ability to accurately identify assault at the time it is occurring (Kahn et al., 2003). These include:

- Relationship with the perpetrator—known assailants confuse victims.
- Use of alcohol or drugs—when alcohol is involved, the victim is less likely to label the experience as rape or abuse.
- Physical force or violence—when no violence is present, abuse is harder to identify.

Relationship to the Perpetrator

These findings make common sense. When a victim is being assaulted by the known abuser, she may feel confused, bewildered, or make excuses for the perpetrator. "He's only like this when he's drunk," "he must've misunderstood," or "he's really not like that" are all things victims might tell themselves to explain the behavior of a perpetrator who is known and loved. If there is a previous consensual sexual relationship, the victim might think that consent is always implied, so that rape is impossible, as in a marriage. The perpetrator can play on this as well. "I thought when you got married, you got all the pussy you want for free," one man testified during a trial involving four marital rapes. Even though he admitted to "taking it anytime" he wanted, he was acquitted.

Not only are victims often confused about what is happening to them, they are confused about the person doing it. Although research-ers label sexual assault by defining the relationship—non-stranger rape, acquaintance rape, date rape—victims are likely to experience the perpetrator of the abuse as a stranger, regardless of the pre-existing relationship. No victim I've ever talked to "knew" that her spouse, friend, or relative was capable of harming her, before the first assault. Even after multiple assaults, many victims have told me, "I just didn't know who he was." The victims did not recognize the rage, cruelty, or indifference to them, not understanding how someone they enjoyed and trusted at some point could harm them. Then, after the offense, the offender returns to "normal," or even to a state the victim sympathizes with, caring for him. As Lundy Bancroft (2002) writes in his book *Why Does He do That*, "looking at him in his deflated state, his partner has trouble imagining that the abuser inside of him will ever be back" (p. 9).

Confusion about the offender and the offender's intent leads victims to engage in rationalizing and excusing the offender's behavior. The victim might tell him- or herself that the offender is "stressed," drunk, depressed, "not himself," good down deep, or other things to explain the offender's behavior. When talking with others, she might insist he is "misunderstood." The victim's psychological and emotional goal is to return that offender to the person that she knows and loves, that she can understand and predict.

Because the victim becomes confused about the offender, she becomes confused about the offender's intentions. A victim may not be able to define the assault as abuse or rape because she may not be able to imagine the offender as an abuser or rapist. Obviously, not only does the victim have to identify the event, here she has to identify the other as a perpetrator of that event. It is easier to attribute the offender's behavior to an accident, misunderstanding, or loss of control rather than to acknowledge the offender's deliberate choices to harm. If a victim is to understand herself as raped or abused, she has to understand her loved one as a rapist or abuser. The grief, loss, and ramifications of labeling another as a rapist or batterer are profound. Additionally, the costs of labeling oneself as a victim, who was vulnerable and out of control, can be profound as well. The victim can adopt and promote the excuses the offender gives.

This type of confusion and disorientation about the event in the offender can contribute to a variety of victim responses. These might include reaching out to the offender to ask why the behavior occurred. Victims often go to the offender to answer questions that only he or she can answer, like "why did you do this to me?" No one else can answer that for the victim. Seeking an explanation, this victim texted her perpetrator, "the man I loved told me I was shit to him and that we weren't even friends. Then he literally beat the shit out of me and told me I was a whore." The man texted back a response: "I didn't beat you."

The victim may provide the offender excuses for his behavior, internally or overtly, that the offender reinforces. After, the offender may apologize, say he was drunk, or act like the event was a misunderstanding. This influences the victim to believe that the assault was a one-time thing or a mistake that warrants neither punishment nor the consequences involved in pursuing prosecution. Neither will label it a crime. She may choose to forgive him, perhaps may even return to the relationship, resolving the confusion by again believing that the offender is the person she loved and liked prior before the event. The victim's process of resolving this confusion can lead to a variety of post-offense behaviors that may be challenging for investigators and prosecutors. She may go to breakfast with the offender. They may go on more dates. She may remain married to him. He may be able to work side-by-side with his abuser the day after the assault. One study of the recantation of victims of intimate partner violence studied prison phone calls between abusers and their victims. Minimizing the abuse, reinvigorating dreams and hopes, and stressing the loss of the relationship and abuser's willingness to change were identifiable tools used by the offender to get the victim to recant the allegations and attempt to drop the charges (Bonomi, Gangamma, Locke, Katafiasz, & Martin, 2011).

Alcohol Use

Alcohol is the drug most commonly associated with sexual assault, whether it is used by the victim or the perpetrator (Grubb & Turner, 2012). Alcohol can be used by offenders to make victims more vulnerable or to facilitate the expression of their own impulses to rape (Valliere, 1997). When alcohol is involved during the time of the assault, a victim becomes more reluctant to label the assault accurately. A woman who has been drinking might blame herself for "getting raped" or, if there was alcohol involved, might not label the attack as rape at all (Kahn et al., 2003). This finding was also true whether or not the male assailant had been drinking.

Not only does research suggest that alcohol use raises a risk of sexual assault, it also supports the premise that sexual assault is taken less seriously when alcohol is involved—not only by the victim but by juries as well. This is true even in cases when the victim was too intoxicated to resist physically (Kahn et al., 2003). Research continues to demonstrate that victims are blamed more consistently when they are intoxicated in a sexual assault than when they are not (Grubb & Turner, 2012). The same authors suggest that victims who were drinking when assaulted are less likely to report the assault.

Absence of Force or Violence

"Well, it was different than the abuse we would talk about. He played with me and gave me treats. I liked it, it was fun, not like what my dad did," explained a 17-year old victim I had treated. She returned to see me after I treated her when she was five, after her father violently beat and sexually assaulted her. She came back at 17 to tell me her foster father was sexually abusing her throughout our therapy. She never disclosed because she did not find it terrifying. If a victim believes that violence is required to define rape or abuse, then "lesser" levels of attack or assault can contribute to a victim's confusion (Littleton et al., 2006). If the victim experiences no injury or does not fear for her life, or does not struggle or fight back, she might believe that she was not "really" abused. A victim of intimate violence might think, "well, he didn't punch me" after being strangled, pushed, restrained, or slapped. A rape victim might also be confused when the offender "just" holds her down, coerces her, or otherwise is unmanageable sexually. This confusion or failure to acknowledge rape could be further compounded if the victim sees the offender's rejection of her refusals as a misunderstanding or blames herself for not being "clear" enough. If she engaged in flirting or some sexual contact prior to a rape, she might think that the offender just didn't realize or "went overboard" with his sexual desires. This excusing of unmanageable male sexual arousal is a significant part of female socialization to sex. One study found that the subjects stated women who were perceived as sexually teasing "deserve" to be raped and victims who saw themselves as teasing did not label their experience as rape (Peterson & Muehlenhard, 2004). The idea of "blue balls" or overpowering lust in males is a theme throughout our society, easily seen in jokes, comments, or even t-shirts. Still, girls and women are held responsible for managing male desire by resisting, not being sexually tempting or attention-seeking, and having to avoid sexual encounters that are not consensual. Over and over again, we hear of victims, "well, what did she think was going to happen . . ." if she dressed like that, went to that place, or drank that much.

Victims who do not acknowledge that they were raped or assaulted not only report less frequently, they have poorer adjustments following the assault. Littleton, Axsom, and Grills-Taquechel (2009) found that unacknowledged victims were more likely to engage in problematic alcohol use, continue a relationship with the offender, and be at greater risk of revictimization. This failure to identify the abuse clearly will affect victim decision-making, whether it is during the assault or after. And it can impact victim behaviors throughout the event. Lack of force or physical violence in a sexual assault is so confusing, it is related to successful acquittal arguments for offenders, even in cases involving sexual assault of very young children (Stolzenberg & Lyon, 2014). Offenders use manipulation, camouflage, and coercion instead of physical violence. Consequently, they are successful at confusing the victim and juries.

A study of incarcerated women found that the women failed to report rape for most of the reasons described above (Heath, Lynch, Fritch,

"Internal Factors" 37

McArthur, & Smith, 2011). The women did not feel they would be believed, could not believe someone they knew could have raped them, blamed themselves for the rape, or failed to identify their experience as rape. Clearly, multiple factors influence a victim's response to assault.

Blame, Shame, and Guilt

Because of many of the issues outlined above, the victim may harbor intense feelings of shame, guilt, embarrassment, or blame for the sexual or physical assault. These feelings may be more intense or exacerbated by the victim's religion, culture, or beliefs. However, the very experience of being assaulted is confusing and humiliating. The victim's physical and emotional integrity has been violated. And the victim has to discuss the assault or abuse in an environment that is infused with victim blaming.

Sources of these feelings may be obvious or subtle. In general, discussing sexual behavior in detail or conflict with a person's loved one is something rarely done at the level that the investigatory process requires. Who put what, where, and when is not something discussed even among closest friends on a regular basis. The investigatory process requires intense examination of every detail of the assault or abuse, requiring the victim to know and face things that are truly unknowable (e.g., "how long did it last?" "How far did it go in?" "What happened, in what order?"). If the abuse is a repeated event, as in the sexual abuse of a child or in domestic violence, the victim has to relive and define many traumatic events or remember discrete details of each event. Each of these reports begs the questions of "why didn't you leave" or "why didn't you tell?" The shame of staying can be overwhelming in the face of judgement from others. "It isn't only that I am ashamed and embarrassed to admit to people what I let happen to me, what I allowed him to do," one victim of emotional abuse explained. "I am ashamed of myself. I mean, what did I let happen to me? Where did I go?" Shame and self-blame play a significant role in labeling the experience as rape or abuse (Peterson & Muehlenhard, 2004), obviously impacting disclosure.

If the victim has an ongoing relationship with the perpetrator, the victim's shame may be in choosing a terrible partner, feeling as though she provoked the partner, the shame of feeling she deserves the abuse, or the shame of facing that this assault might not be the first or third or tenth. Revealing the abuse may begin an exploration of the history of violation in the relationship. An investigation of a sexual assault may include an examination of the victim's sexual or other behavior. For example, a victim might have to describe how she knows the anal penetration this time was different than the consensual times. Or how behaviors that were allowed with one partner were not allowed with another. He might have to talk about infidelity or why he allowed one act but felt raped after

38 Victim Response to Interpersonal Violence

another act. "Well, I mean, we were into rough sex, it was our thing," the victim of rape said. "But this was different. He really hurt me on purpose."

Sexual response to an assault can have the consequence of creating confusion and shame, as can being unsure if the sexual contact was unwanted. If the victim responds physiologically to an assault or if the offender uses the response against the victim, the victim might be confused about consent or the offender may claim consent as a defense (Levin & van Berlo, 2004). Orgasm, erections, genital stimulation, and lubrication can occur during an assault. It should be noted by all prosecutors that unwanted sexual arousal is completely possible; a defense based on the victim's sexual response as proof of consent should be completely dismissed (Levin & van Berlo, 2004). Another issue is the victim's sense of her own consent. If the victim is not sure whether or not she would have consented to sex if she could have (e.g., intoxication), she might not label her experience as rape (Peterson & Muehlenhard, 2004). "I mean, I would have said yes, I liked him," a young woman told me. "But then he just started doing it to me. What was that?" Even more confusing is a perpetrator who will use coercion when cooperation is available

It is important to ask and explore with the victim not only what the victim believes she is to blame for, but what she fears the investigator, prosecutor, or jury will blame her for. Not only will this allow accurate reassurance and intervention to occur, it will also allow the victim to explain this to the jury. In the context of fears and self-blaming beliefs, behavior becomes much more understandable.

Vulnerability and Weakness

A woman arrives in a city strange to her. Her flight had been delayed. The people assigned to pick her up left hours before. She has no way to her hotel. A man pulls up to the curb and offers her a ride. She accepts with relief after he assures her that he knows where her hotel is and will take her there. Instead, he drives her to an isolated area and rapes her.

Many people who hear this story wonder how the victim could have made such a bad choice. A strange man? Getting into a strange car? The victim's choices are examined and questioned. Why did she make herself so vulnerable? In reality, this story simply reflects a taxi or Uber ride with an unexpected outcome. The vulnerability caused *by the victim's decisions* is the focus of our attention and is readily highlighted during the prosecutorial process.

Being assaulted necessitates a revelation that the victim was vulnerable. Being a victim is itself a shameful experience. There is implied weakness and failure in the term "victim"—so much so that some victims reject the word, resulting in the adoption of words like "survivor." The victim may have to discuss choices that he or she regrets, like drinking too much, kissing too many people in the bar, or throwing up after drinking. The victim's self-evaluation comes first, then the victim has to subject him- or herself to the evaluation of others. This does not happen typically with even our most foolish decisions, as we have some control over the privacy of the consequences of our choices. Victims of assault who enter the process do not.

Given that, victims are acutely aware of the choices made that contributed to the situation they were in. Mostly we evaluate choices that a victim made in the context or understanding that the end result was a rape or battering. We Monday morning quarterback the events in hindsight. The victim engages in that retrospective evaluation as well, bemoaning different choices. It is critical to understand and reiterate to the victim that the choices were made *without the knowledge that the consequences would be an assault*. Obviously, if the victim knew that at the end of that day, that relationship, that dinner, she was going to be raped or battered, her choices would've been different all along. It is a distorted way of analyzing a situation retrospectively in the context of a consequence that could not have been anticipated.

Despite the distorted inaccuracy of this method, it is still done by victims, investigators, and attorneys throughout the process and is even utilized by the offender to influence both the victim's perception and the community's perception of the victim's choices. Additionally, offenders understand that is highly effective to get victims to cooperate with their own offenses. The more choices a victim makes along the way to be with, engage with, or provide opportunity to the perpetrator, the more a victim is likely to blame him- or herself for the outcome and the perpetrator's actions.

Victim choices that result in vulnerability are readily labeled "bad" or "stupid" decisions. Inability to leave an abuser, needing love and acceptance, fearing loneliness or loss of love are all things that people deem "weak." Victims are often "diagnosed" with low self-esteem, so end up feeling damaged, deserving of maltreatment, and somehow wrong and worthy of the poor treatment the abuser has meted out. The victim's sense of self is a clear internal factor that can impact the accurate labeling of abuse as well as help-seeking decisions.

Prior History of Abuse/Assault

A very high portion of victims who are physically or sexually assaulted have a prior history of physical or sexual assault. Being a victim of abuse puts someone at significant risk of being abused again in the future; in fact, it is the strongest predictor of future victimization. This has been demonstrated over and over in the research (Classen, Palesh, & Aggarwal, 2005; Turchik et al., 2009; Casey & Nurius, 2005). In a review of the literature, Classen and colleagues (2005) found that two out of three people victimized as children will be victimized again. This finding is true for both homosexual and heterosexual victims (Balsam, Lehavot, & Beadnell, 2011). This is very important for investigators and prosecutors to understand. It directly contradicts the notion that "lightning never strikes twice in the same place," which can result in an inaccurate conclusion that the victim was lying, exaggerating, or "cries rape" on everyone. One child I treated had eight perpetrators. She was placed repeatedly in the care of the perpetrators after disclosing because the caseworkers concluded, "no one gets abused that much."

How does this impact a victim's response to sexual assault? It would be convenient if a prior history of abuse made victims better able to protect themselves, identify perpetrators, identify abuse, or react decisively when faced with another abusive episode. Unfortunately, that is not typically the case. A prior history of assault can be a significant factor in the victim's pre-offense behavior, behavior during the offense, and post-offense behavior. Although Kahn et al. (2003) found that women abused as children acknowledged later assaults as rape more often, their risk of being revictimized did not decrease. A history of abuse can make it more difficult for victims to assess or detect risk, teach victims that resistance is futile, or contribute to a sense of recklessness and self-destructive behavior that increases the victims' chances of being assaulted, as well as ineffectively protecting themselves or resisting (Norris, George, Stoner, Masters, Zawacki, & Davis, 2006; Turchik, Probst, Chau, Nigoff, & Gidycz, 2007).

Victims of abuse can have many responses to trauma that makes them more susceptible to future abuse (Classen et al., 2005). They may engage in risk-taking behavior, including substance abuse or indiscriminate sexual behavior. They may have a poor ability to judge what is normal and healthy in intimate relationships. They may struggle with hyper-reactivity in fear of conflict. They may have internalized a distorted notion of love, intimacy, and relationships that include the tolerance for certain level of abuse. They may have prior experiences where they were not believed or supported. "I don't know—I didn't think he loved me if he wasn't so passionate and jealous. That's the way it always was. I know it was abuse now and some back then, but I always thought it was desire," a victim of childhood abuse told me about her abusive partner.

Being assaulted, especially if the abuse was repetitive, may have taught the victim a number of things about him- or herself and perpetrators. The victim of ongoing abuse might have learned that resistance is futile, offenders are unmanageable, or that "just lying there" gets it over with more quickly. The victim may have developed coping strategies that include dissociation or depersonalization—psychological terms for "checking out" during the offense so that the experience is minimized. Dissociation as a coping skill is more common in repeated traumas (Classen et al., 2005). "I just wanted it to stop, so I just laid there and cried," many victims have told me. The victim may have been trained to be passive during an offense or have learned to placate and please the offender in order to avoid more harm. "If I didn't hold still, he would bite my penis," one boy told me. "Fighting back just made it worse." A victim may have adopted a position of learned helplessness, when nothing she can do influences the behavior of the offender. Finally, a prior history of abuse may lend to the victim's terror response, resulting in tonic immobility, or physiological freezing, during the offense. Victims who have been previously abused are more likely to respond with immobility (Campbell, 2012).

If the victim's prior abuse created a traumatic reaction, the victim might have a trauma-related disorder or suffer from other negative effects, like depression, anxiety, or somatic (physical) issues (Whiffen & MacIntosh, 2005). She might have a history of self-abuse or problematic interpersonal reactions that make her ashamed, socially isolated, or vulnerable psychologically (Whiffen & MacIntosh, 2005). Many of the offenders I have worked with discover quickly whether a person they are targeting have been previously abused, selecting specifically for that vulnerability. Offenders know to prey on the issues related to trauma, like the susceptibility to attention, isolation, failure to perceive risk, and need for love that victims might present. Substance abuse is common in victims of assault as well, increasing the offender's access to her.

Finally, a victim may use their prior experience to compare their current situation to and evaluate the definition of abuse. For example, one child I worked with was sexually assaulted and beaten by her violent, crack-addicted father through her childhood. While in therapy with me as a very little girl, we talked about her terror, the pain, in the fear she experienced. Unfortunately, years later, she returned to therapy to talk about the sexual abuse she was experiencing at the hands of her foster father during the time of our therapy. She did not understand that what he was doing was abuse at the time. He was kind and playful. He gave her candy and affection. He sexually stimulated her, so the assaults felt good to her. She loved him, a feeling she did not have for her father. This child waited over a decade to report these assaults because she could not identify this abuser and these actions as the abuse she had previously experienced. Many victims of abuse compare abusers, thinking the new person is "not as bad as" a previous abuser.

As an investigator, it is important to know your victim's prior history and their experience of that, without assumptions. The victim might be able to describe the process of dissociation or the decision-making process and how she relied on past experience to guide her through her current assault. Prosecutors can also use the victims' reactions as proof that she did not experience a consensual encounter. Being disconnected

Socialization to Aggression and Conflict

We are all socialized differently to violence, aggression, and conflict. This socialization interacts with our internalized ideas of gender as well. Even in my work with trained soldiers, who are likely to have been socialized toward aggression much more specifically than most victims of violence, they will respond in their own personal comfort zone with a level of aggression or conflict during an assault. Females, in particular, are socialized to keep the peace and be nice and passive. This impacts their ability to respond to assault (Turchik et al., 2007).

It is important to understand how a victim views violence or conflict, especially in the context of a relationship with an abuser. There are so many potential influences of the socialization to nonaggressiveness, passivity, being nice, or keeping the peace—impacting behavior during the assault itself through to the prosecution process. Remember, too, the prosecution process is one of the most direct confrontations and conflict-laden situations that can exist.

During the assault, a victim has to decide to fight. This decision is influenced by identification of the attack, willingness to harm the attacker, belief in the effectiveness of fighting, and past history of success. The victim has to identify an attacker as an enemy. In most anyone's socialization to aggression, aggression is sanctioned when it is aimed at a defined enemy, whether in sports or in war. Otherwise, aggression is discouraged. For some, it is taboo. It can take strenuous effort to override these internal barriers to aggression. Gender roles and socialization make these barriers bigger. Even now, females are encouraged to be gentle, conciliatory, and placating, while males are encouraged to be aggressive. In fact, aggressiveness in females is considered a negative, resulting in pejorative labels like "bitch." Following an assault, a victim might be socialized to make up, be friendly, or not cause trouble. Some religious beliefs require forgiveness or "turning the other cheek." Reporting the assaults to authorities could confirm the perpetrator's assertion that the victim is a "vindictive bitch" who just wants to see him hurt. The offender can play on this as well. One rapist complained about a victim who didn't respond to him "cheering her on" to complete a competition, openly questioning her "attitude" to others. He didn't bother to add that this "attitude" occurred the day after he raped her. Another confronted a victim he raped and strangled about why she was so "bitchy" and not "appreciative" of the personalized birthday present he left her after the assault.

"Internal Factors" 43

Experience with conflict might impact confrontation in a marriage or love relationship. A victim might have an expressive family to whom yelling and talking out problems is common; yet, confronting her battering husband results in assault. Her many experiences with being able to work things out by arguing could lead her to repeated assaults by her husband, which he then blames on her for "pushing his buttons" and failing to "shut up."

Prosecutors must remember that the process of prosecution is conflictual by nature. Understanding how the victim views justice, punishment, and conflict can provide an appreciation for the barriers the victim might be facing as a part of the process, as well as how others might perceive her behavior, including participation in the process.

Fear of Penalization

> *I wasn't going to tell anybody. I mean, I worked as a medic. He worked there too. I heard how people talked about 'victims.' It was terrible. And I heard how they talked about him. Everyone loved him. I didn't want everyone to hate me.*
>
> *—Victim of rape by a coworker who did not disclose for 8 months*

Penalties for telling are real in the world of a victim. There are innumerable losses and risks for disclosing all types of abuse. We have discussed the countless ways that victims can blame themselves and be blamed by others for the assaults; however, victims are blamed and penalized for a great many other things following reporting the abuse. A victim who is not initially believed by law enforcement could even face prosecution for false reporting (Armstrong & Miller, 2017).

First, if a victim is in a relationship with the offender, the victim can be blamed for the loss of the offender and consequences to the offender, like jail, the dissolution of the family, the family's financial ruin, or for bringing shame onto the family. "If you had only told me first, we could have handled it in the family," victims are told. Recent high-profile cases evoke harsh, contemptuous condemnation of victims, labelling them liars, gold diggers, or attention seekers (and these are the nice things). For telling, children may be placed in foster care. They may lose contact with their other parent, who might choose to stay with the offender. They may be penalized by siblings, who are angry with and hateful toward them for "ruining everything." The penalties might include money, time, loss of work, loss of loved ones, or emotional penalties, like being shunned by members of the family. "Yeah, she doesn't talk to her sister anymore. She doesn't know her nephews. Most of the family cut her out and they weren't even related to me," one rapist told me. He had abused his

44 Victim Response to Interpersonal Violence

sister-in-law from ages 10 to 16, then again when she was 19. When she finally reported, the family turned against her. The offender was convicted and served years in prison. However, the victim still wasn't embraced by her family and remained isolated. The messages that the victim gets include, "well he needs help, not jail. You didn't have to go that far." One only has to examine social media responses to victims to find evidence of the consequences of telling.

Retaliation against victims is quite real as well. Victims are negatively labeled. People take sides against the victim, aligning with the perpetrator, labeling the victim a liar, and blaming the victim for consequences to the offender. Victims are blamed for the offender's loss of career and status. The retaliation may be as direct as the courthouse confrontations in the I have witnessed or as insidious and persistent as comments on Facebook or other social media. Victims tend to be avoided and socially ostracized. As one victim said to me, "there are sympathy cards for everything—death, cancer—but there are no sympathy cards for rape. No one even wants to acknowledge it has happened." If you want to get a true sense of the pervasiveness and cruelty of retaliation, read comments below articles on convictions for assaults or follow social media for the victims or perpetrators. After a high-profile conviction of a West Point cadet for rape, the comments included calling the victim a liar, highlighting all the victim's choices and behaviors, and making assertions that the cadet was not "a man like that." Participants blame politics for the conviction, warning men to get out of the Army. I myself have received threats, been called terrible names, and been professionally demonized for my Tedx talk regarding sexual assault. This was retaliation merely for discussing victims and vulnerability.

Offenders are quite aware of the penalties for telling. In fact, they might intentionally use these against the victim. "You don't want daddy to go to jail, do you," an offender might ask his child, ensuring that that child doesn't tell. Other tactics include saying "mommy will be mad at us," scapegoating the victim in the community, or eroding the victim's supports and credibility prior to disclosure, so that when the victim told, she would not be believed. "I talked to Scott and Shawn about how, you know, Julie doesn't love me anymore, how she don't have the feelings for me anymore," one offender admitted, setting up his friends to believe she would make a false allegation against him. Domestic violence offenders might tell others how their wife is crazy, vindictive, bipolar, or unfaithful, so when the allegations occur, people are primed to believe they are false.

Victims may not anticipate the consequences of telling either, resulting in recantation and incredibly frustrating experience for investigators and prosecutors. The good news is that awareness of the potential penalties for telling allows helpers and prosecutors to institute appropriate support and possibly mitigate some of the penalties, as well as protect the victim from retaliation with appropriate court orders or community sanctions for retaliation.

Summary

All victims carry many factors within them that influence their behaviors and decisions before, during, and following assault or abuse. These factors even enable or disable a victim from accurately labeling the assault as an assault. When these things are explored and explained to a jury by the victim, the behaviors become more understandable. An expert in victim dynamics can assist prosecutors in explaining these issues as well. Good communication with the victim and an exploration of the areas discussed can define the context of the victim—the internal world that guides how the victim sees and interacts with the external world.

In conclusion:

- Many internal factors impact victim decision-making. These include:
  - Fear;
  - Cognitive Biases;
  - Cultural factors;
  - Religious factors;
  - Beliefs and values;
  - Confusion about the assault;
  - Self-blame and shame;
  - Prior history of abuse or assault;
  - Socialization to aggression or conflict; and
  - Fear of penalization for reporting.
- These factors not only impact the victim's decision-making or behaviors during the offense, they can profoundly affect the victim's participation in the prosecutorial process.
- Some of these factors can also have a complicated impact on the victim's adjustment post-offense, again affecting the victim's ability to participate in the prosecution of the offender.
- An informed investigator prosecutor can play an important role in anticipating the barriers the victim faces and providing effective intervention to assist the victim with these barriers.
- The victim, with appropriate preparation and understanding of the issues, can provide education to juries or factfinders regarding the decision. An expert witness can also be useful in educating juries or factfinders regarding victim dynamics and the internal factors that play a role.

46 Victim Response to Interpersonal Violence

References

Ariely, D. (2008). *Predictably irrational: The hidden forces that shape our decisions*. New York: Harper Collins, Inc.

Armstrong, K., & Miller, T. C. (2017, November 24). When sexual assault victims are charged with lying. *New York Times*. Retrieved from www.nytimes.com

Balsam, K. F., Lehavot, K., & Beadnell, B. (2011). Sexual revictimization and mental health: A comparison of lesbians, gay men, and heterosexual women. *Journal of Interpersonal Violence, 26*(9), 1798–1814.

Bancroft, L. (2002). *Why does he do that? Inside the mind of angry and controlling men*. New York: Berkley Books.

Baron, J. (2007). *Thinking and deciding* (4th ed.). Cambridge: Cambridge University Press.

Bonomi, A. E., Gangamma, R., Locke, C. R., Katafiasz, H., & Martin, D. (2011). "Meet me at the hill where we used to park": Interpersonal processes associated with victim recantation. *Social Science & Medicine, 73*, 1054–1061.

Brafman, O., & Brafman, R. (2011). *Sway: The irresistible pull of irrational behavior*. New York: Doubleday.

Campbell, R. (2012, December 3). The neurobiology of sexual assault. *An NIJ Research for the Real World Seminar*. National Institute of Justice: US Department of Justice. Retrieved from www.nij.gov/multimedia/presenter/presenter-campbell/Pages/welcome.aspx

Casey, E., & Nurius, P. (2005). Trauma exposure and sexual revictimization risk: Comparisons across single, multiple incident, and multiple perpetrator victimizations. *Violence Against Women, 11*(4), 505–530.

Classen, C. C., Palesh, O. G., & Aggarwal, R. (2005). Sexual revictimization: A review of the empirical literature. *Trauma, Violence, and Abuse, 6*(2), 103–129.

Coxwell, A., & King, M. (2010). Adult male rape and sexual assault: Prevalence, revictimization, and the tonic immobility response. *Sexual and Relationship Therapy, 25*(4), 372–379. doi:10.1080/14681991003747430

Cuevas, C. A., Sabina, C., & Picard, E. H. (2015). Posttraumatic Stress among victimized Latino women: Evaluating the role of cultural factors. *Journal of Traumatic Stress, 28*, 531–538.

Edwards, J. (Reporter). (2017, April 24). *Breakdown: Predator MD* (Episode 4). [Audio podcast]. Retrieved from www.myajc.com/news/state--regional/breakdown-s03-doctor-relocates-his-practice-and-his-problem/

Flood, M., & Pease, B. (2009). Factors influencing attitudes to violence against women. *Trauma Violence Abuse, 10*(2), 125–142. doi:10.1177/152483800 9334131

Gardner, D. (2009). *The science of fear: Why we fear things we shouldn't and put ourselves in greater danger*. New York: Penguin.

Grubb, A., & Turner, E. (2012). Attribution of blame in rape cases: A review of the impact of rape myth acceptance, gender role conformity and substance use on victim blaming. *Aggression and Violent Behavior, 17*(5), 443–452.

Heath, N., Lynch, S., Fritch, A., McArthur, L., & Smith, S. (2011). Silent survivors: Rape myth acceptance in incarcerated women's narratives of disclosure and reporting of rape. *Psychology of Women Quarterly, 35*(4), 596–610. doi:10.1177/0361684311407870

Hilbert, M. (2012, March). Toward a synthesis of cognitive biases: How noisy information processing can bias human decision making. *Psychological Bulletin, 138*(2), 211–237. doi:10.1037/a0025940

Hopper, J. (2018, September 5). Why it's time for sexual assault self-defense training. *Psychology Today*. Retrieved from www.psychologytoday.com

Kahn, A., Jackson, J., Kully, C., Badger, K., & Halvorsen, J. (2003). Calling it rape: Differences in experiences of women who do or do not label their sexual assault as rape. *Psychology of Women Quarterly, 27*, 233–242. doi:10.1111/1471–6402.00103

Kahneman, D. (2011). *Thinking fast and slow*. New York: Farrar, Straus and Giroux.

Kozlowska, K., Walker, P., McLean, L., & Carrive, P. (2015). Fear and the defense cascade: Clinical implications and management. *Harvard Review of Psychiatry, 23*(4), 263–287. doi:10.1097/HRP.0000000000000065

Lerner, M., & Simmons, C. (1966). Observer's reaction to the innocent victim: Compassion or rejection? *Journal of Personality and Social Psychology, 4*(2), 203–201.

Levin, R. J., & van Berlo, W. (2004). Sexual arousal and orgasm in subjects who experience forced or non-consensual sexual stimulation. *Journal of Clinical Forensic Medicine, 11*, 82–88.

Littleton, H., Axsom, D., Breitkopf, C., & Berenson, A. (2006). Rape acknowledgement and postassault experiences: How acknowledgment status relates to disclosure, coping, worldview, and reactions received from others. *Violence and Victims, 21*(6), 761–778.

Littleton, H., Axsom, D., & Grills-Taquechel, A. (2009). Sexual assault victims' acknowledgment status and revictimization risk. *Psychology of Women Quarterly, 33*, 34–42.

Norris, J., George, W. H., Stoner, S. A., Masters, N. T., Zawacki, T., & Davis, K. C. (2006). Women's responses to sexual aggression: The effects of childhood trauma, alcohol, and prior relationship. *Experimental & Clinical Psychopharmacology, 14*(3), 402–411.

Peterson, Z., & Muehlenhard, C. (2004). Was it rape? The function of women's rape myth acceptance and definitions of sex in labeling their own experiences. *Sex Roles, 51*, 129–144.

Peterson, Z., & Muehlenhard, C. (2011). A Match-and-Motivation Model of how women label their nonconsensual sexual experiences. *Psychology of Women Quarterly, 35*(4), 558–570. doi:10.1177/0361684311410210

Russo, F. (2017, August). Sexual assault may trigger involuntary paralysis. *Scientific America*. Retrieved from www.scientificamerican.com/article/sexual-assault-may-trigger-involuntary-paralysis

Stolzenberg, S., & Lyon, T. (2014). Evidence Summarized in attorney's closing arguments predicts acquittals in criminal trials of child sexual abuse. *Child Maltreatment, 19*(2), 119–129. doi:10.1177/107755951453988

Turchik, J. A., Probst, D. R., Chau, M., Nigoff, A., & Gidycz, C. A. (2007). Factors predicting the type of tactics used to resist sexual assault: A prospective study of college women. *Journal of Consulting and Clinical Psychology, 75*(4), 605–614.

Turchik, J. A., Probst, D. R., Irvin, C., Chau, M., & Gidycz, C. (2009). Prediction of sexual assault experiences in college women based on rape scripts: A prospective analysis. *Journal of Consulting and Clinical Psychology, 77*(2), 361–366.

Valdovinos, M., & Mechanic, M. B. (2017). Sexual coercion in marriage: Narrative accounts of Mexican-American women. *Journal of Ethnic & Culture Diversity in Social Work, 26*(4). doi:10.1080/15313204.2017.1300437

Valliere, V. (1997). Relationships between alcohol use, alcohol expectancies, and sexual offenses in convicted offenders. In B. Schwartz & H. Cellini (Eds.), *The sex offender: New insights, treatment innovations, and legal developments–Volume II* (pp. 3-2–3-14). New Jersey: Civic Research Institute.

Volchan, E., Souza, G., Franklin, C., Norte, C., Rocha-Rego, V., Oliveira, J., . . . Figueira, I. (2011). Is there tonic immobility in humans? Biological evidence from victim of traumatic stress. *Biological Psychology, 88*, 13–19. doi:10.1016/j.biopsycho.2011.06.002

Whiffen, V. E., & MacIntosh, H. B. (2005). Mediators of the link between childhood sexual abuse and emotional distress: A critical review. *Trauma, Violence, and Abuse, 6*(1), 24–39. doi:10.1177/1524838004272543

Wilson, L. C., & Miller, K. E. (2016). Meta-analysis of the prevalence of unacknowledged rape. *Trauma, Violence, and Abuse, 17*(2), 149–159. doi:10.1177/1524838015576391

Chapter 3

"Where Was I Supposed to Go?"
External Factors That Influence Victim Response and Help-Seeking

Really? It was 2:30 in the morning. I didn't want to get a DUI or walk through the neighborhood alone after being raped. Was I going to call my mother, so far away? I had to just wait a little while there.
—Victim of assault, after being asked why she did not immediately leave her assailant's home

Not only is the victim's decision-making guided by the internal factors that the victim brings with her or him to the assault or abuse, there are many external factors that can dictate a victim's behavior. External factors are those things outside the victim that impact and guide a victim's behavior and decision-making. Even when a victim is emotionally ready to address her assault or abuse, her choices might be dictated by many social, economic, or practical realities. These can include limitations on services or supports, dependence on the abuser, pressure by others, a lack of social support, or being in a closed system with the abuser. There may be children involved. There may be unconsidered practicalities that the victim is attempting to negotiate while dealing with the assault itself.

Additionally, it is important to recognize that victims are less likely to seek formal help that might result in investigation and prosecution than they are to seek informal help, from friends and supports (McCart, Smith, & Sawyer, 2010). This results in the under-reporting of assaults of all types. Understanding what barriers might exist to help-seeking, as well as the informal sources of help, will assist the investigator of reported assaults.

Access to Services

On the face of it, access to services appears to be a relatively simple thing to assess. Basically, can the victim get help or get to help, or not—right?, I often have seen this issue assessed on a very basic level. Victims are scrutinized because they have had phone calls with family, went to school,

50 Victim Response to Interpersonal Violence

knew where the behavioral health center was, had access to a car, or other examples following an assault. Why didn't the victim go for help? Yell? Escape?

In reality, access to services is a very complicated thing to assess. In regard to help-seeking, an investigator or prosecutor must explore a variety of issues before categorizing the victim's behavior simply as a failure to seek help. Exposing the barriers to help-seeking is critical to helping the jury or judge understand the victim as well as to reveal the complex behavior and influence of the offender. It is also important to understand that there are differences between *formal* services and *informal* services. Formal services include law enforcement, professionals, or prosecution, while informal services include friends, spiritual guidance, and family.

> *"I knew I would never go for help," she explained. "I also heard how the people there talked about victims. They trashed them. Everyone was lying according to them. I wasn't going to be a victim."*

This statement was from a victim who waited eight months, suffering severe post-traumatic symptoms after a rape by a coworker, to disclose and the get medical help she needed. She had significant anal injuries that did not heal. Despite the injuries and the destructive impact her secret had on her marriage, the victim did not seek help because she worked in the same hospital to which she would need to go for treatment. Her experience of her coworkers precluded her help-seeking. Another victim, a child who was being tortured, was taken to the doctor monthly. He attempted to tell his psychiatrist once, with dire consequences.

> *After she would hurt me, she would take me to the doctor. She would tell them how bad I was, how I would hurt myself . . . She took me to [the psychiatrist] every month. He never talked to me alone. She would always tell him I was out of control. I even told him she was abusing me, two times, once right in front of her. He didn't believe me. She could always talk him out of it. She beat me up when we got home.*

The offender can be the biggest barrier to services for the victim. The offender might check mileage, control the victim's independence, or isolate the victim from seeking help. The offender might threaten the victim with consequences for disclosing or have previously alienated her from those who could help. In some cases, the assault might have occurred where the only services available were from the offender or the offender's support system. The offender might appear unpredictably, insist on accompanying the victim everywhere, or otherwise block access to services, like withholding an insurance card. Help-seeking might expose the

"External Factors" 51

victim to being discovered in an attempt to escape. In one case, a perpetrator tracked down an escaping victim through the child's medical assistance card.

The inability to access services might be purely practical. If the abuser controls the money, the victim might not be able to escape an abusive relationship. If there is a language barrier for the victim, she might rely on the perpetrator to interpret or be the conduit for services. This was the case in one brutal abuse and rape case I testified about. The victim was Spanish-speaking in a rural Pennsylvania community. When she would call for help, the law enforcement had to rely on the perpetrator to communicate with the victim, as there were no interpreters or Spanish-speaking officers available. In fact, research shows that language barriers are significant for Hispanic clients accessing services and help-seeking (Rizo & Macy, 2011). Victims in rural areas have limited resources. Victims in small communities might not believe they will have privacy, confidentiality, or protection when the family or offender is known throughout the community. In fact, Logan, Evans, Stevenson, and Jordan (2005) found that in victims in rural communities, privacy issues and fear of family backlash were significant. Limited availability of quality services contributes to poorer outcomes for victims in rural communities as well (Edwards, 2015). Victims whose abusers are law enforcement or involved in the criminal justice system face the same practical barriers (Friedersdorf, 2014). It seems likely that a generalization of these issues in closed communities (rural, law enforcement) could be made to other similar communities, like the military.

The LGBTQ community faces particular issues in accessing services (Calton, Cattaneo, & Gebhard, 2016). A victim in a same-sex relationship might be legally barred from obtaining protection orders. They might be ignored or discouraged from services by law enforcement. Obtaining justice through prosecution for a member of the LGBTQ community might be very difficult, as it requires overcoming attitudes that deem the abuse or rape of a victim from this community as less serious. Shelters are much less available. Many of these same things are true for male victims of sexual assault, who underreport tremendously, are likely to be blamed for the offense, and lack the availability of services for men (Davies, 2002).

Barriers to Help-Seeking During the Offense

It is important to understand a victim's decision-making, during an assault, regarding help-seeking. Superficially, a victim's decisions or failures to get help might lead to a belief that the victim was participating in a consensual act or lying about the assault. When a victim answers a text from a friend after being raped or talks on the phone with her mother after being assaulted without disclosing, it can cut against her credibility if not

52 Victim Response to Interpersonal Violence

well understood or explained. A simple exploration of the issues often provides a legitimate rationale for the victim's behavior.

A victim I know was raped by her estranged husband. He raped her in her room in a way that was perfect for prosecutors—injury, break-in, ripped clothing, immediate reporting, interest in prosecution. However, the prosecutor questioned her after finding out that other people were in the home. Why didn't she yell for help? On the face of it, that question is relevant. It became irrelevant when the response was that the "people" at home were the offender's grandchildren. The victim's primary concern was protecting the children from being a witness to her sexual assault by Pop-Pop.

It is essential to know if the victim believed she could actually get help. Were the people around children? Was it a parent 400 miles away? Was it someone who was aligned with the perpetrator? Was it someone that the victim needed to protect physically or emotionally? It is possible that the victim does not even know how to get to the location she is at, especially if the perpetrator has removed her from a familiar environment. It is also possible it is 3:00 a.m. and no one is available. Being caught texting for help could alert the abuser that the victim is help-seeking, provoking the offender and increasing the victim's danger. The goal of the victim is to get through the assault as quickly and safely as possible. A victim often has very clear and rational decision-making regarding a decision not to reach out for help.—it could truly be useless. A text to someone far away could only serve to upset the other, who is rendered helpless. If the victim does not know where she is or what the address is, a call is useless.

Also, the very nature of sexual assault is private. I have worked with victims who have been raped in a hotel room with others sleeping in the next bed. The victims' choice to be silent was to protect themselves from being seen naked by others, prevent exposure of the humiliation of the assault, or attempt to maintain some semblance of control of the situation. Sometimes, as we have discussed, the victim is not even entirely sure if an assault is occurring. Until the victim has clarity about the event, crying for help is not a consideration.

Who could potentially help is an important issue. A victim might not choose to seek help because the people present are supporters of the offender. One victim of an assault in a fraternity house did not yell for fear that the others would possibly become involved in the assault, cheer on the offender, or humiliate her. She did not know the other fraternity brothers. Another adolescent victim was raped in the basement of the offender's home. The person from whom to get help was the offender's mother. The victim was not supposed to be at the home in the first place. It is critical to investigate the factors that present barriers to the victims' help seeking.

"External Factors"   53

The victim's decisions can be explored by an interviewer with some insightful questions: What kept you from calling for help? What made you decide not to scream? Was there anyone you thought could help you? What did you think the attacker would do if you got your phone? These are all the types of questions that can reveal the thought processes that lead the victim to choose what she did, resulting ultimately in her survival.

Presence or Protection of Witnesses/Children

Often offenses or abuse occur in the home, especially in cases of domestic violence or intimate partner assault. Victims, even those experiencing heinous assaults, will prioritize the protection of others or witnesses for many reasons. The witness might become a victim. For example, children will attempt to intervene with abuse and become a target (Bancroft, Silverman, & Ritchie, 2012). Or a witness might be dragged into the investigation or prosecution process. In domestic violence, abusers who are escalating can be assaultive toward family members of the victim. In intimate partner assaults, up to one-half of child witnesses get involved in the violence. When a gun is involved, most of the time, children are present. Children are more likely to be abused in a home where there is domestic violence (Bancroft et al., 2012). During an assault, a victim might not cry out or attempt to escape an assault for fear of leaving children with the abuser or of exposing the child to violence.

Victims might not seek help in an effort to bar the offender from harming others. Offenders are often a threat to third parties. Abusers of children might threaten the victim's mother, siblings, or pets. In fact, protection of pets can control a child or keep a domestic violence victim from leaving an abuser (Bancroft et al., 2012). A child victim might endure sexual assault in the belief that she is protecting a younger sibling from being sexually assaulted. "I thought if I just did it, he wouldn't go after her," one child told me. Another boy provoked his stepfather, eliciting beatings with the belief that he was distracting the abuser from his mother and sister. When he found out that his sister had been raped by his stepfather, he could not believe it—his sense of shame and failure was overwhelming. "If I believe her," he said, "it means I took it all for nothing. I couldn't stand knowing that."

A mother in the home with an abusive partner will remain in the relationship to protect the children. She might fear that the abuser will take custody or abduct the children. In fact, batterers win custody battles with significant frequency (Bancroft et al., 2012; Chesler, 2011). Abduction of the children is a real threat (Bancroft et al., 2012). The mother might fear that the children will be unprotected and abused during visitation when the abuser has the children alone. She might fear financial devastation and poverty for the children, loss of their health insurance, or loss of their life stability (e.g., having to change schools or homes). The need to protect for the victim can occur in the immediacy of the assault or over the course of time for the witnesses or children.

Opportunity for Escape

Potential for escape is a topic that is highlighted extensively during the prosecution of assault. Why didn't he run? Why did she stay after and sleep in his bed? In fact, in the cases of Jaycee Dugard and Elizabeth Smart, the media repeatedly focused on the fact that the victims would go places in public with the offender, never seeking escape. Elizabeth Smart cited "her survival instinct" (Stump, 2017). Jaycee Dugard stated, "I knew there was no leaving" (Kearney, 2011).

First, it is critical to understand that escape, or the possibility thereof, is something we *always* evaluate after the fact. If an offender goes out for pizza after raping a victim and is gone for 20 minutes, it is clear in hindsight that the victim had an opportunity to call a cab, run out, text, or do whatever behaviors could be deemed escaping the situation with a rapist. But remember, this is hindsight. When we judge a victim's response, we are doing it *after the fact, with all the information.* In that moment, the victim did not know it would be 20 minutes, experiencing the offender's absence on minute at a time. The victim might be in shock, have nowhere to go, or be reliant on the offender for transportation. The victim might not know where she is, have no money for a cab, or not want to antagonize the offender. Some victims fear that leaving is a test. Another possibility is that the victim is simply relieved the worst is over, feeling that the danger has passed and that it is safe now. Remember, too, that escape might not be necessary or possible for the victim as a result of physiological issues or, as will be discussed in the next chapter, the victim's experience with the offender.

Experience With and Revictimization by Law Enforcement or the Criminal Justice System

Victims experience significant barriers to help-seeking specifically involving the criminal justice system and law enforcement in particular. Victims still experience being blamed for the attack, having their behaviors investigated and questions, and being shamed by law enforcement. Rural victims tend to be negatively impacted by a lack of resources, fear that the law enforcement officers might know the perpetrator, or the stigma and shame in a small community (Edwards, 2015). The relationship between help-seeking with law enforcement and sexual identity is significant. Victims from the LGBTQ community can face stigma, can be

"External Factors" 55

arrested as the perpetrator, or may be harassed and discriminated against by law enforcement (Calton et al., 2016; Sable, Danis Mauzy, & Gallagher, 2006). Stalking, a dangerous behavior associated with violence and sexual assault, is often minimized by law enforcement, especially when there is a prior relationship between the perpetrator and victim (Weller, Hope, & Sheridan, 2013).

Law enforcement officers play a critical role in the reporting, investigation, and prosecution of interpersonal violence. They are often the first responder to the victim and play a key role in whether or not the case is referred for prosecution. They make initial decisions on "victim credibility." A victim's perception of the legitimacy of law enforcement is very important in victim cooperation and formal help-seeking. If a victim perceives law enforcement officials as willing to follow the law, treat her fairly, and follow through with investigation, her cooperation and willingness to report is increased (Koster, 2016). However, the opposite is also true: if the victim feels that the perpetrator will be favored or more valued or if she distrusts the system, her cooperation and willingness will decrease. Unfortunately, a recent survey by the National Domestic Violence Hotline in 2015 revealed that victims of domestic violence "showed a strong resistance" to utilizing law enforcement. More than one-quarter of victims said they would not call police, one-half thought police would make it worse, and more than two-thirds thought police would not believe them or would do nothing (National Domestic Violence Hotline, 2015). Secondary victimization by law enforcement is a prevalent experience; those who experienced secondary victimization were unlikely to have the cases prosecuted, while victims who described law enforcement as compassionate were more likely to have cases successfully prosecuted (Patterson, 2011).

Being in law enforcement does not make one immune to acceptance of rape myths. Victims themselves face their own acceptance of myths, overcoming them to make reports to law enforcement. However, a recent study demonstrates that law enforcement not only continues to accept rape myths, but that this acceptance appears in official police reports. Both blaming the victim and denying the assaults on the basis of victim behaviors were documented in official statements (Shaw, Campbell, Cain, & Feeney, 2017). The reports reflected a victim's failure to resist, lack of injury, victim's emotional presentation, or victim intoxication all as reasons to doubt the victim's credibility. A survey of Sexual Assault Nurse Examiners demonstrated their belief that officers revictimize victims by failing to ask questions in a sensitive way, failing to proceed with investigations, and asking victim blaming questions (Maier, 2012). Police in another study were more likely to support victims who matched their expectations of a rape victim and whose assaults were more severe and more likely to be prosecuted (Anders & Christopher, 2011). Police did not offer adequate support to sex workers or other victims who had engaged in criminal behavior, reinforcing those victims' reluctance to report. The good news from this study is that support by police had a significant influence on the victim's choice to proceed to prosecution.

The criminal justice system poses issues beyond law enforcement. The victim might not understand the system, might fear consequences for his or her own behavior, or might believe that the abuse was not a crime or that the offender does not deserve jail. Collateral consequences for victims might be significant. A college student might get expelled for reporting a rape after she was underage drinking or using drugs. A soldier might receive consequences for fraternization or other problematic behavior. A prostitute who is raped might be arrested for prostitution. In fact, in a recent case I worked, a woman appeared at police drugged and battered to report she was being sex-trafficked. She was arrested for prostitution. The perpetrator went on to have four more victims (at least) that he was arrested for and continued to try to traffic women while incarcerated. Fear or threat of deportation can prohibit undocumented women from reporting abuse (Rizo & Macy, 2011). Gay and bisexual students faced expulsion for reporting rape at the Mormon-owned Brigham Young University (Bahadur, 2016).

Even if the victim reports and participates in the investigation, the chances of the offender being prosecuted are slim. Statistics cited by RAINN, the Rape Abuse Incest National Network, demonstrate that not only is sexual assault underreported but that when it is, only nine out of 1,000 rapes makes it to prosecution—and only five cases will lead to a felony conviction ("The Criminal Justice System," 2019). Along the way, the victim has to talk about the assault in minute detail over and over again. Hopefully, the prosecutor or trial team, including the advocate, will not change jobs or leave in the process.

The criminal justice process is particularly hard during trial. Again and again, I have to remind prosecutors that they are not defending the victim, but prosecuting the offender. It is so difficult to shift the paradigm in assault cases to be offender-focused, especially when the typical focus of defense is the victim's behaviors and choices. Revictimization can occur in the system when charges are not filed, cases are postponed repeatedly, or unsatisfying plea bargains are accepted by prosecutors (Maier, 2012).

Despite all the potential negative effects that law enforcement and the criminal justice system can have on victims, a positive experience with the system can help ensure future reporting. When a victim has confidence in the response of law enforcement, she is more likely to report future violence. When follow-up calls are made or law enforcement continues contact with the victim, she is more likely to report revictimization. Studies show clear implications for improving system response to victims to better facilitate prosecution and decrease secondary trauma (Shaw et al.,

"External Factors" 57

2017; National Domestic Violence Hotline, 2015; U.S. Department of Justice NIJ Special Report, 2009).

Consequences of Reporting

Although many prosecutors and helpers experience relief and elation when abuse is reported or successfully prosecuted, we sometimes fail to see the profound consequences of the reporting. A child who might tell about abuse to his friend may be in foster care the next day, without a family, his pets, his school, or his friends. A victim might have to reveal her mental health history, sexual history, or even financial history. Although not all of it might appear during trial, she is still investigated. My recent trials have forced victims to discuss balances on credit cards, prior abortions, consensual sexual practices of bondage, or medications for mental health issues. Not only are victims forced to disclose the most intimate details of the crimes ("Where did he ejaculate?" "Where did you spit it?"), but their lives, thoughts, feelings, and choices also are under a microscope. When calling for help, there are many potential unintended consequences. A victim might be arrested for reporting, as the primary aggressor or in states that have mandatory arrest policies. A perpetrator might face losing a job simply because police responded.

These issues do not even begin to cover what the victim faces for reporting. There is lost time at work, childcare issues for interviews and trial, the impact on the family, and now with social media, the commentary of the public. But perhaps the most powerful issues include consequences to others, including the offender; fear of retaliation; and the experience of loss.

Consequences to Others/Offender

"Well, I worried and I was sad. I worried about what it would do to my family. I worried about taking Nicholas' father away. I mean, he was good, a good father. I didn't want to hurt my mother," she explained, trying to describe how she made the decision to keep her abuse by her stepfather a secret. Another victim stated, "he was the best we had, the best medic. We were in theater. What was I going to do, jeopardize the whole unit?" In another case, the pediatrician served women and children on medical assistance. He gave good care to the underprivileged and their babies, but he assaulted the women who came to his office. What were they to do? In all of these cases, the reporting had dire consequences to others.

A victim bears the burden not only of the trauma of the abuse, but also the decision to report and all its ramifications. A child has to decide if she wants to put her dad in jail. The Sandusky victims had to choose whether to jeopardize the status and success of Penn State. A man has to decide whether to lose his lover and his dreams of the future together. Although it is always the offender who has made the initial choice, the victim bears the weight. Often, victims are told to "keep it in the family" or just "get help" rather than seek assistance in the criminal justice system. Year in and year out, offenders confront me or my staff on why we are keeping them from their children or enforcing restrictions on them, as if they did not choose the abuse or assault with the risks that came with it. This feeling of protecting the offender increases when the victim loves the offender and time has passed. In a fascinating study analyzing prison phone calls between abusers and their victims, a clear pattern emerges, showing how the offender can gain the victim's sympathy, get the victim to align with him, and activate the victim's protection against the system, ultimately leading to the victim's recantation (Bonomi, Gangamma, Locke, Katafiasz, & Martin, 2011).

A victim with children in a domestic assault situation faces many choices regarding the protection of children. Calling police could result in the children's direct exposure to the assault or the exposure of the children to a volatile arrest. I have treated children who witnessed police "taking down" their father or having their father call to them for help while in handcuffs. Children can easily be targeted during the violence and more than one-half of children become directly involved in the violence (Bancroft et al., 2012). Calling police or seeking help for victims of intimate partner violence could result in other consequences, like having the children removed by child protective services (Davies, Block, & Campbell, 2007). It is important to remember that children are witnesses as well and can be co-opted or targeted by the abuser. In many cases I have been involved in, the victim makes extraordinary choices to protect children—laying silently while being raped brutally so as not to wake the baby sleeping next to her in the bed or offering sex to a violent partner so he would not throw scalding coffee at the table where the baby sat in the high chair. When children are present during an assault or if they rely on the victim or perpetrator for care, the game changes altogether.

Protection of the offender's career can place tremendous pressure on the victim. Recent examples of athletes who have beaten their wives or committed sexual assaults and the exposure of the Catholic Church highlight this issue clearly. Not only is the victim responsible for the impact on the offender's career, but on the society or community as a whole.

Again, the victim bears the burden of the consequences of reporting. She has to decide how the children will be impacted without a father or at school if other kids find out. He has to decide if reporting the rape by his lover will destruct the offender's family when the offender is outed. The victim might weigh the offender's sickly mother, who could die while he was in jail, in her decision to prosecute. Unlike the offender, the victim

"External Factors" 59

is generally focused on all these facets of reporting while the offender has already made the choice to offend.

Retaliation

Retaliation towards victims is a very real phenomenon. Offenders are a significant source of both the retaliation and the victim's fear of retaliation, using threats to significantly influence victim response. However, retaliation comes from many sources and has a profound impact on the victim. Retaliation can be formal or informal, professional or social. In a recent survey, RAINN reported that fear of retaliation was cited by 20% of victims of crime ("The Criminal Justice System," 2019).

Retaliation towards whistleblowers and those who report sexual harassment has been studied formally. In her testimony to the U.S. Judicial Proceedings Panel, Dr. Lilia Cortina described her findings on retaliation toward victims reporting sexual assault ("Victim Retaliation," 2015). The forms of retaliation included the overt, such as unfairly poor job performance reviews and denials of promotions, and the subtle, such as victims being given less favorable job duties or transferred. The measurable social/informal retaliation included being shunned, gossiped about, or ignored. All of these impacts affect a majority of the victim's daily life. To report sexual harassment or sexual abuse at work, a victim has to face threat of losing her job, of being labelled a troublemaker, and of not being hired elsewhere if a reputation of "causing problems" or "making accusations" precedes her. Dr. Cortina's study showed that 66% of those reporting faced social retaliation and 36% faced both social and professional retaliation. Retaliation decreases well-being and job satisfaction as well ("Victim Retaliation," 2015). Citing another study done by the U.S. Equal Employment Opportunity Commission in 2016, Golshan (2017) reported that 75% of those who reported workplace abuse faced retaliation.

Considering that sexual harassment is sexual offending, just within a public forum, it would not be surprising to find that these results are generalizable. The victims of Harvey Weinstein, Bill Cosby, and other high-profile, powerful figures faced retaliation, tremendous scrutiny, and evisceration over social media. In fact, Harvey Weinstein was quoted as saying to a victim, "one call and you're done" (Towhey, Kantor, & Dominus, 2017). Although that reflects the power of the offender, it also *reflects the confidence the offender has in his community to carry out retaliation.* Up to 65% of service members in the military reported some form of retaliation after reporting sexual assault. Members reported being harassed, attacked, or physically assaulted by fellow service members in retaliation for reporting (Childress, 2015). On top of that, punishment for retaliation is rare, if ever. Victims whose offenders are gang members, have extended family who are aligned with the offender, or who are popular on campus or on the unit not only must fear the offender, but also his supporters as well. Any future victims who witness retaliation learn about the consequences of reporting also.

Loss

As discussed in the first chapter, loss is one of the most—if not the most—painful human experiences. Although it is easy and simple to focus on the victim's safety, freedom from pain and abuse, and chance to heal in these cases, it is important to understand and acknowledge the tremendous grief and loss that goes with reporting abuse and pursuing prosecution.

Loss is practical as well. If the abuser is the primary income earner, the family can be put into poverty. Even if the victim can work, childcare might become an issue. There is loss of status, standard of living, extended family, friends, and even communities. A military spouse who is involved in a court martial against a soldier spouse will have to leave the Army, leave the community, and leave all their friends and resources to return to the civilian world. Recently, in a case of a serial rapist and batterer who trafficked his victims, his victimization of his girlfriend came to light. She had inherited a significant amount of money. He convinced her to buy a home and put his name on it. When he began beating and raping her, she could not get him to leave her home. A year went by; she still was not in her home and the prosecution was going nowhere. She dropped the charges in exchange for her home. Even calling the police can get a victim evicted if the landlord deems the abuse a problem (Covert, 2015).

Remember, loss aversion is one of the most—if not the most—powerful forces in decision-making (Kahneman, 2011). When a decision is considered from the standpoint of losing something rather than the standpoint of gaining something, people typically and naturally will avoid loss. Some of the things we say to victims have to do with what they will gain by participation in the investigation or the prosecution of the abuser, like freedom, safety, well-being, closure, or justice. These things are not as salient as potential or real losses.

Societal Messages

Retaliation, victim blaming, excuses for offenders, and "rape culture" all convey to victims societal messages and beliefs, not only regarding sexual assault or domestic violence, but about victims, women, offenders, and the reporting itself. Retaliation is instigated at least in part through the community's belief that the offender is the true victim and the victim is perpetrating a lie against the abuser. There are many beliefs promoted in society, easily seen in articles, quotes, and social media:

- The victim lied for attention, money, or revenge;
- "Crying rape" is an easily and often used weapon of women;
- Boys will be boys and rape is a "boy" behavior;
- The victim asked for, allowed, or provoked the abuse/assault;
- There is shame in being a victim;
- General and varied misogyny;
- Victims are "complaining," weak, or can't "deal with it;" and many, many others.

Simply googling "rape meme" or domestic violence jokes will reveal how society views and tolerates assaultive behavior. Instantly visible are Bill Cosby memes about sexual assault, the "rape sloth" meme, and memes about "domestic violence awareness," promoting the ideas that most domestic violence is instigated by women. Recently, even the current President of the United States said that it was a "dangerous time for men." Societal messages include cultural and regional messages about assault or violence. They include messages about systems, "us versus them" mentalities, and ideas about the environment of the victim like assumptions about sexual and drinking behaviors of college students. These attitudes play well in the courtroom, with jurors finding their attitudes and myths echoed in questions and arguments of the attorneys. Prosecutors must dispel these myths, reminding everyone that there is no such thing as a "rapeable offense" or an action that "deserves a beating."

Even less blatantly destructive messages are conveyed societally. These might include stereotypes about offenders that contradict the victim's abuser; for instance, if the offender is not ugly, poor, criminal, or otherwise "that guy." The idea that it is important to keep family problems private can impact a victim. The insidious stereotypes of victims as damaged, incapable, masochistic, or pathetic affects victims. When I train, I often ask my audience how their perceptions of my status, credibility, or professionalism would be shaped if I were to disclose that I was a current victim of domestic violence. Participants admit that they would wonder what was wrong with me and doubt me as a trainer. The victim's willingness to embrace the label of being a victim is a complex process that requires a discarding of the social messages to be quiet and conform.

Support System of Victim

Social support is one of the most important factors in victim response to assault, both negatively and positively. The impact of social support networks, or lack thereof, is cited as the primary factor in predicting reporting of assault, participation with the investigation and prosecution, and in the development of PTSD. When the supports are good, there is a much better outcome. Good support from family and friends was a very significant factor in a victim's decision to aid prosecution of a sexual assault (Anders & Christopher, 2011). However, when supports are negative, it can be devastating to the victim and the investigation and prosecution.

Victims of violence are more likely to seek support or help from informal sources like friends and family than from formal sources like law enforcement (McCart et al., 2010). However, the response of the informal support system can be critical in determining whether the victim pursues formal help and engages in the investigation and prosecution of crime, as well as seeking mental health services (Davies et al., 2007). Davies et al. (2007) found that women who felt supported were more likely to contact police after an assault. In another study, rape survivors' decision to report was directly related to support of family, friends, social service providers, and police, with the caveat that these supports did not subscribe to rape myths (Anders & Christopher, 2011). In direct contrast, children who are not believed about an assault by their primary caretaker, typically the mother, are much more likely to recant the allegations of abuse (Malloy, Lyon, & Quas, 2007).

Social support can mitigate the development of PTSD in victims of intimate partner violence (Dutton, 2009) or during other traumatic events (Clapp & Beck, 2009; Dinenberg, McCaslin, Bates, & Cohen, 2014; Robinaugh et al., 2011). Being a victim of intimate partner violence is associated with traumatic disorders, suicidality, and other issues with functioning. Abusers often socially isolate their victims. Not only are these victims experiencing traumatic events, they also are robbed of the mediator for the development of worsening symptoms and the primary factor in seeking help and intervention. Clearly, offenders benefit in multiple ways from socially isolating the victims.

Social media might prove to be an important source of support or retaliation for the victim in your case. Recently, I was involved in a case where a victim of child sexual abuse in her church disclosed in a group on Facebook. There was an outpouring of support, including some from the church, validating her memories and helping her identify the man who assaulted her. The same can be true for negative social response as well. In another case, the attacks on the case and victim in the comment section of news story about the assault were brutal. Discussing social media with the victim might be important, both in understanding the role of social media for the victim and for the offender.

Assessing, activating, and utilizing the victim's support system is critical in the investigation and prosecution process. A skilled prosecutor will take full advantage of the victim advocate as well as communicate with the victim's primary support system where possible. However, do not assume that all supports are equal. For instance, although a victim's mother might be willing to accompany the victim through the process, that might not be what the victim wants. Fear of exposure, embarrassment and shame, or a conflicted relationship might inhibit the victim's testimony or disclosure. The victim's need to protect a parent might come into play. The victim's mother might blame the victim or be so emotional that the victim ends up caring for the parent. I have seen this in case after case. In one trial, a victim's mother was invited and assumed to be part of the victim's support system. Not only did the victim and mother have a very ambivalent and conflicted relationship, but the victim's mother never supported her Army career, spending part of her time bad-mouthing the service and lamenting the victim's choice to anyone who would listen. Another time, a prosecutor engaged a victim's mother, not knowing she was still married to another perpetrator of the victim after not believing the victim's allegations in the past. In other cases, someone the victim had identified as a "best friend" eventually testified for the offender, disclosing private information about the victim that had been disclosed during the friendship.

Other Post-Offense Influences on Victim Response

There is not an exhaustive list of all the things that can impact a victim's response to an assault. Many more external factors can have a bearing on whether or not the victim resists, reports, or cooperates with criminal justice process. Consider the following when attempting to understand the victim:

- *Third parties*—Are there third parties who are pressuring the victim? Are the children begging for their father or relatives urging the victim to keep family matters private? Is the victim seeking support from a relative of the offender who was "like a sister?" Is there another authority guiding the victim's decisions, like an elder or pastor?
- *Time*—How much time has passed between the offense and what you need from the victim? Have there been repeated continuances? Time can be a crucial issue, especially if the victim faces repeated disappointments or has other life contingencies. The injuries might have healed and are not long-visible proof. Additionally, time has passed for the offender as well. The victim might be aware that the offender has "found Jesus" and repented. The offender might have gotten messages to victim through the family or engaged in a campaign to discredit the victim. Pretrial confinement might convince the victim that the offender has "suffered enough" or paid the consequences.

- *Pressure to return to normal*—Victims can be pressured by others or circumstance to "get back to normal." They have to be parents, coworkers, family members, and members of their community. Sometimes that requires them to put aside their trauma or losses and get on with it. Revisiting and reliving the assault can disrupt their normal functioning. If enough time has gone by, the victim might be in a new relationship, move, or have a baby. The victim might struggle introducing the terrible event into the new life she or he has built.
- *Costs of prosecution*—It does not pay to be a victim of a crime. There are real financial costs to victims, including loss of work, costs for travel, and costs to privacy. It is difficult for a victim who wants privacy to give reasons why he or she needs to take off work to participate in a trial. Imagine if a victim has kept his sexuality private and has to testify in a battering or sexual assault case. The costs of prosecution go beyond money. The victim can be subject to intense scrutiny and exposure during a trial where the public could be allowed to be present.

Summary

External factors that sway victim responses range from the immediate to the far reaching, the practical to the subtle. Some of these factors are systemic, entrenched in the way we think about and do things. Luckily, we can have some influence on this, doing things in a way that is better for victims and better for the likelihood of prosecution. A victim will likely respond well to an interviewer who can anticipate and name the barriers the victim faces. This interviewer or prosecutor will convey knowledge, experience, and empathy. That person will also decrease the victim's defensiveness and sense of being judged.

Remember:

- Barriers to help seeking exist both during and after the assault;
- Access to services can be more complicated than it appears, especially to victims who have ongoing relationships with the offenders;
- Many barriers are created by the victim's wish to protect and care for others;
- A victim's behaviors are evaluated in hindsight without regard to the reality of the moment, as in an assessment for a victim's opportunity to escape;
- Law enforcement plays a crucial role in how a victim proceeds with a report of an assault and cooperation with the prosecutorial process;
- There are significant, sometimes dangerous, consequences to reporting for the victim, including retaliation and loss; and,
- Social support is tremendously important for the victim's decision-making and navigation of the system following an assault.

The good news is that we can improve our response to victims by knowing these factors. Utilization of a victim advocate, knowing the resources available to victims, and being a positive social support for the victim can all profoundly help your case. The more barriers you can remove or minimize, the more likely the victim will remain involved. This sometimes can be done by a simple phone call with information for the victim or to check in with him or her. It can be done by ensuring that information and training about the issues described is available for those involved including law enforcement, advocates, prosecutors, and others. You increase the likelihood of cooperation of victims by proactively addressing some of the hurdles that they face.

References

Anders, M., & Christopher, F. (2011). A socioecological model of rape survivor's decisions to aid in case prosecution. *Psychology of Women Quarterly, 35*, 92–106. doi:10.1177/0361684310394802

Bancroft, L., Silverman, J., & Ritchie, D. (2012). *The batterer as parent: Addressing the impact of domestic violence on family dynamics*. Los Angeles, CA: Sage.

Bahadur, N. (2016, October 13). Want to know why women don't report sexual assault? *Self*. Retrieved from www.self.com/story/why-women-dont-report-sexual-assault

Bonomi, A. E., Gangamma, R., Locke, C. R., Katafiasz, H., & Martin, D. (2011). "Meet me at the hill where we used to park": Interpersonal processes associated with victim recantation. *Social Science & Medicine, 73*, 1054–1061.

Calton, J., Cattaneo, L. B., & Gebhard, K. (2016). Barriers to help seeking for lesbian, gay, bisexual, transgender, and queer victims of intimate partner violence. *Trauma, Violence, & Abuse, 17*(5), 585–600. doi:10.1177/1524838015585318

Chesler, P. (2011). *Mothers on trial: The battle for children and custody*. Chicago, IL: Lawrence Hill Books.

Childress, S. (2015, May 18). How the military retaliates against sexual assault victims. *Frontline*. Retrieved from www.pbs.org/wgbh/frontline/article/how-the-military-retaliates-against-sexual-assault-victims/

Clapp, J., & Beck, J. (2009). Understanding the relationship between PTSD and social support: The role of negative network orientation. *Behaviour Research and Therapy, 47*(3), 237–244. doi:10.1016/j.brat.2008.12.006

Covert, B. (2015, August 27). When calling the police on an abusive partner leads to a victim losing her home. *ThinkProgress*. Retrieved from https://thinkprogress.org/when-calling-the-police-on-an-abusive-partner-leads-to-a-victim-losing-her-home-96e068990d9f

"The Criminal Justice System: The Statistics." (2019, April 29). Retrieved from www.rainn.org/statistics/criminal-justice-system

Davies, K., Block, C., & Campbell, J. (2007). Seeking help from police: Battered women's decisions and experiences. *Criminal Justice Studies, 20*, 15–41. doi:10/1080/14786010701241317

Davies, M. (2002). Male sexual assault victims: A selective review of the literature and implications for support services. *Aggression and Violent Behavior, 7*, 203–214.

66 Victim Response to Interpersonal Violence

Dinenberg, R., McCaslin, S., Bates, M., & Cohen, B. (2014). Social support may protect against development of posttraumatic stress disorder: Findings from the heart and soul study. *American Journal of Health Promotion, 28*(5), 294–297. doi:10.4278/ajhp. 121023-QUAN-511

Dutton, M. A. (2009). Pathways linking intimate partner violence and post-traumatic stress disorder. *Trauma, Violence, and Abuse, 10*(3), 211–224. doi: 10.1177/1524838009334451

Edwards, K. (2015). Intimate partner violence and the rural-urban-suburban divide: Myth or reality? A critical review of the literature. *Trauma, Violence, & Abuse, 16*(3), 359–373. doi:10.1177/1524838014557289

Friedersdorf, C. (2014, September 19). Police have a much bigger domestic violence problem than the NFL does. *The Atlantic.* Retrieved from www.theatlantic.com

Golshan, T. (2017, October 15). Study finds 75 percent of workplace harassment victims experienced retaliation when they spoke up. *Vox.* Retrieved from www.vox.com/identities/2017/10/15/16438750/weinstein-sexual-harassment-facts

Kahneman, D. (2011). *Thinking fast and slow.* New York: Farrar, Straus and Giroux.

Kearney, C. (2011, July 11). US kidnap victim Dugard says why she couldn't escape. *Reuters.* Retrieved from www.reuters.com

Koster, N. (2016). Victims' perception of the police response as a predictor of victim cooperation in the Netherlands: A prospective analysis. *Psychology, Crime, & Law, 23*(3), 201–220. doi:10.1080/1068316X.2016.1239098

Logan, T., Evans, L., Stevenson, E., & Jordan, C. (2005). Barriers to services for rural and urban survivors of rape. *Journal of Interpersonal Violence, 20,* 591–616.

Maier, S. (2012). Sexual assault nurse examiner's perception of the revictimization of rape victims. *Journal of Interpersonal Violence, 27*(2), 287–315. doi:10.1177/0886260511416476

Malloy, L., Lyon, T., & Quas, J. (2007). Filial dependency and recantations of child sexual abuse allegations. *Journal of the American Academy of Child & Adolescent Psychiatry, 46*(2), 162–170. doi:10.1097/01.chi.0000246067.77953.f7

McCart, M., Smith, D., & Sawyer, G. (2010). Help seeking among victims of crime: A review of the empirical literature. *Journal of Traumatic Stress, 23,* 198–206. doi:10.1002/jts.20509

National Domestic Violence Hotline. (2015). *Who will help me? Domestic violence survivors speak out about law enforcement responses.* Washington, DC. Retrieved from www.thehotline.org/resources/law-enforcement-responses

Patterson, D. (2011). The linkage between secondary victimization by law enforcement and rape case outcomes. *Journal of Interpersonal Violence, 26,* 328–347. doi:10.1177/0886260510362889

Rizo, C., & Macy, R. (2011). Help seeking and barriers of Hispanic partner violence survivors: A systematic review of the literature. *Aggression and Violent Behavior, 16*(3), 250–264.

Robinaugh, D. J., Marques, L., Traeger, L. N., Marks, E., Sung, S., Gayle Beck, J., . . . Simon, N. (2011). Understanding the relationship of perceived social support to post-trauma cognitions and posttraumatic stress disorder. *Journal of Anxiety Disorders, 25*(8), 1072–1078. doi:10.106/j.janxdis.2011.07.004

Sable, M., Danis, F., Mauzy, D., & Gallagher, S. (2006). Barriers to reporting sexual assault for women and men: Perspectives of college students. *Journal of American College Health*, *55*, 157–162.

Shaw, J., Campbell, R., Cain, D., & Feeney, H. (2017). Beyond surveys and scales: How rape myths manifest in sexual assault police records. *Psychology of Violence*, *7*(4), 602–614.

Stump, S. (2017, November 14). Elizabeth Smart on the one question that won't go away: Why didn't you run? *Today*. Retrieved from www.today.com

Towhey, M., Kantor, J., & Dominus, S. (2017, December 5). Weinstein's complicity machine. *New York Times*. Retrieved from www.nytimes.com/interactive/2017/12/05/us/harvey-weinstein-complicity.html

US Department of Justice. (2009). *NIJ special report: Practical implications of current domestic violence research: For law enforcement, prosecutors, and judges*. Retrieved from www.ojp.usdoj.gov/nij

Victim Retaliation: Hearings before the Judicial Proceedings Panel. April 10, 2015. (testimony of Dr. Lilia Cortina). Retrieved from http://jpp.whs.mil/topic-areas/victim-retaliation

Weller, M., Hope, L., & Sheridan, L. (2013). Police and public perceptions of stalking: The role of prior victim–offender relationship. *Journal of Interpersonal Violence*, *28*(2), 320–339. doi:10.1177/0886260512454718

Chapter 4

"I Will Not Be Denied"
Influence of the Offender on Victim Behavior

The biggest lie was convincing them how important they were to me. Because they weren't really that important to me—to get them to think that they were really special a special person to me, a special part of my life and I needed them to be there—that was the biggest lie.
—Offender of adult and child victim

He would just do it or would pout or have a fit until I submitted. Sometimes, when he had my dick in his mouth, he would wiggle up until his penis was in my face. I knew what that meant—he wanted me to suck him. I would turn my head away—then he would bite my penis. You can only take so much, so I would open my mouth and let him in.
—Victim of child sexual abuse

Often ignored, but profoundly important, is the offender's influence on victim response. In case after case I have been involved in, the victim's choices have been examined or explained in a vacuum without addressing how the offender instigated or manipulated the victim's response. As we know, most people are sexually or physically assaulted by someone they know, with whom they are in an ongoing relationship. That allows the offender intimate knowledge about the victim and the victim's responses, ways of coping, and vulnerabilities. It allows the offender to engage in long-term actions that prepare the victim to be a victim of a crime or to control the victim's response after the offender commits a crime.

The offender also controls the environment around him- or herself and the victim. Offenders engage in many behaviors that are instrumental in controlling others' perception of the abuser, the victim, and the situation. In fact, if an offender can successfully manage the perceptions of those around them, that offender can effectively and repeatedly get away with criminal acts of abuse. For example, one offender I worked with used to call the police on himself. When police would respond, he would drunkenly and tearfully complain about his troubled stepdaughter who caused so many problems in the household. On one occasion, the girl disclosed to police that her stepfather had been raping her. The officer left the home, patted the offender on the back, and lamented with him, "I see what you have to put up with here. You won't believe what she accused you of." The offender estimated that he had done this around 50 times, sometimes after the victim's disclosure, before someone believed the victim. He also admitted he had been sexually assaulting the child for years before her disclosure. She had repeatedly tried to tell without success.

It is often so unbelievable to people that offender is capable of controlling the victim and those around them, or the "audience" to the offense, that we attempt to understand and explain the victim by using terms like "victim dynamics" or "counterintuitive victim behavior." I would argue that victim dynamics are, in fact, normal responses to an offender's influence in an abnormal context—the context of abuse. In my years of working with offenders and victims, the only ones who do not question the victim's behavior are offenders. They not only anticipate the victim's responses, but they count on them. "I just didn't think they would tell . . . because they looked up to me, thought I was cool, because they wanted to continue drinking . . . they would think they would get themselves in trouble," explained an offender who was a former attorney, regarding his confidence on how he could hide his behavior. Another offender explained how he would fix things with his victim after assaulting her. "I would sit on the bed and cry," he said. "I would hand her the phone and beg her to call the police on me, telling her she didn't deserve what I did. She never called." This offender knew that his victim's love for him and care for his well-being would prevent her from calling the police and would facilitate her forgiveness.

The offenders rely on common techniques to manipulate the victim and the environment. Even in situations in which the offender has a brief relationship with the victim, offenders engage in behavior to ensure their success at getting away with a crime. A study by Katz and Barnetz (2016) examined children's descriptions of offender behavior. The children described a consistent process of manipulation by the abuser: Build attachment, manipulate the victim's family, tempt or coerce the victim, abuse the victim, then tempt and coerce again to prevent disclosure. This course of conduct is applicable to all types of victims when the offender has ongoing access to that victim. The following is not an exhaustive list of things the offenders do to achieve their goals, but they are behaviors commonly seen in crimes of interpersonal violence.

Influence on the Victim

In general, we are familiar with the concrete and practical ways that the offender can influence and control the victim. It important to assess the more overt means of controlling and influencing victims in your cases

70 Victim Response to Interpersonal Violence

or investigations. An offender can have status, power, or the means to damage the victim physically or socially. A partner can control finances, socially isolate the victim, or threaten the victim with viable threats. A parent can use the fear of losing a child against another parent to control behavior and reporting. A loaded weapon in the house or against the head of a victim will clearly dictate the victim's reactions. Financial or social losses and dependency on the offender seem to be more easily accepted explanations for victim behavior than the more subtle and complicated psychological and emotional manipulations of the victim.

Getting the Victim to Cooperate: Why Did She Allow It?

> *Most people who brainwash . . . use methods similar to those of prison guards who recognize that physical control is never easily accomplished without the cooperation of the prisoner. The most effective way to gain that control is through subversive manipulation of the mind and feelings of the victim . . .*
>
> —Amnesty International Report on Torture, 1975, pg. 53

"I mean, they had all the choices. I gave them all the decisions. Who were they going to tell on? Themselves?" an offender of 96 adolescent boys once said to me. He was explaining why no victim told on him, highlighting one of the most sophisticated and essential elements involved in controlling all human behavior—gaining cooperation. As humans, we generally like to cooperate, especially with someone we have interest in or feel affinity for, like a loved one, friend, coworker, or even a date. Cooperation is easily achieved by offenders, who then use the victim's choices to blame the victim for the outcome.

Examples are numerous. In fact, almost all defense arguments in sexual assault cases involve highlighting the victim's cooperation with the offender. These things can include a victim's decision to drink, trust the offender, stay in the home, get in a car, give the offender a phone number, return a text to the offender, engage in some sexual behavior before the assault, and on and on. The most effective offenders will not use force, coercion, or violence when it is not necessary, when the victim is going along with the offender's wishes. This is true in sexual assault and intimate partner violence. An abuser in the home who can gain the victim's compliance by a look, signal, or threat is less likely to escalate to physical violence (unless that is what will gratify that offender). Once a victim has made choices to accommodate or engage with the offender, the offender can hold the victim responsible for the outcome. "Well, she could have fought back, I mean, how was I to know?" one offender asked me after describing his victim's turned head and tears during an assault.

"Influence of the Offender" 71

Another offender explained his assault of his grandchild, saying, "I mean, she would run right up and hug me! She asked me to rub her back! To me that meant she wanted it!" "She knows how I get," a domestic violence offender stated. "When will she learn not to argue with me!"

Not only do offenders hold the victims more culpable for the outcome of the decisions, the victims themselves do. Most of us who have worked with victims hear this in their self-blame: "if only I hadn't . . ." "I don't know why I allow him to do this to me . . ." "I should have listened . . ." are some examples. The more a victim feels responsible for the assault, the less likely he or she is to report the crime or engage in help-seeking. Not only does the victim blame herself, we blame her too. "What did she think was going to happen," "how could he be so stupid," or other victim blaming statements highlight this phenomenon. We even have colloquialisms that reflect this idea as well. "Don't poke the bear," "don't swim with sharks," or others are used to dismiss the offender's culpability for assaultive behavior and blame the victims. Cooperation of the victim always benefits the offender.

Identifying and Exploiting Vulnerability

Offenders are incredibly good at identifying and exploiting vulnerabilities and their victims. They are able to pick out victims with particular personalities. "I really liked her sister more, but she was a loudmouth. [The victim] was quiet," the offender explained, going on to describe how he tested her by making her keep secrets before the assault. In another case, a mother of two victims highlighted her third child's personality as a protective factor. "I don't think Shamar was abused," she told investigators. "He is very loud and honest. I don't think he would have allowed it to happen. He would have been loud." Offenders identify pre-existing circumstances in victims that will contribute to the success of the offense behavior. Social isolation, poor reputation, substance abuse, mental health issues, poor job performance, or other vulnerabilities can contribute to an offender's selection of the victim. A victim may simply be kind, trusting, or lonely. These normal human characteristics can be manipulated into vulnerabilities for an offender.

Vulnerabilities can give the offender access to the victim, increase the likelihood that the victim will become involved with the offender, and decrease the likelihood that the victim will be believed.

> On top of that, I knew the dynamics that were going on in her household. Her parents were divorcing, she was youngest child. I was the youngest child so I know the constant need of being accepted and all of a sudden I took her under my wing and made her feel like she was part of something bigger—I always sat back on that.

The offender explained how he chose his victim and what vulnerabilities he used against her to gain her trust and access to her. Another offender explained, "I knew they wouldn't tell." He went on to describe how he knew this: "I remember making distinctions between different kids so the ones that I provided alcohol to were the ones with less connections to their parents, got along less with their parents. I knew who the good kids were." A violent offender explained how he chose his next partner. "She told me her ex was abusive. I made sure that I never did the same things. Then I could say I wasn't as bad or blame her because she was the common denominator," he said. Socks were the target of another offender's attention. He would look at children's socks to see if they were dirty, worn out, mismatched, or missing. He had learned that children who were not well cared for often had issues with socks.

It is important to remember that victim vulnerabilities are not weaknesses or a way to blame the victim or explain the offender. The truth is, there is no vulnerability without danger. Being with someone dangerous who will rape or harm the victim is the problem—not that the victim drank too much, had mental health issues, was too dependent, or had any other issue exploited by the offender. When investigating or prosecuting a case of assault, the offender's exploitation of vulnerability should be highlighted, not the vulnerabilities themselves. At each point, a person can offer care, comfort, or resources to a vulnerable person rather than harm her or him, as an offender chooses to do.

Another point to keep in mind is that being sexually assaulted or physically abused causes some of the very issues that offenders can exploit. Abuse and trauma can cause a victim to have mental health issues, to engage in criminal or high-risk behavior, to abuse substances, or to be otherwise dysregulated. A victim may be irritable, depressed, angry, or have health problems. Someone being abused may not do well in school, work, or in their military service. The very nature of having to keep abuse secret creates a liar out of the victim. All of these issues that the offender and the abuse create, the offender benefits from when a disclosure or report is made. When possible, while guarding the victim's legal rights, it is important to have the victim explain the connection between the psychological and behavioral issues the victim is struggling with to the offender's behavior.

Building Attachment

Not only do offenders prey on vulnerabilities, like intoxication, poor reputation, or social isolation in their victims, they create vulnerabilities. I like to point out that offenders weaponize the human frailties of love, trust, and hope in their victims. Many offenders work diligently to get their victims attached to them in one way or another, building upon and exploiting affection, attention, love, or need. This can be as sophisticated as getting a victim to fall in love with them or as simple as gaining access to a victim alone by being nice enough to drive them someplace.

"I think I was giving something to him that he didn't have, something I was fulfilling even though it was wrong," the former priest told me. "It was not good for him. I think he thought somebody was caring about him, had feelings towards him." He went on, "we did a lot of fun things that sort of replaced the bad things." Despite the abuse, relationships with offenders can have many benefits. The person could be the victim's battle buddy, best friend, or favorite cousin. Remember, by the time helpers get involved in the relationship between the abuser and victim, we have the benefit of hindsight. We know the costs to the victim, the tragedy of rape and battering, and the character of the offender. We have clarity because the offender has not garnered our affinity, provided us comfort, or been in control of our relief from pain or trauma.

Being Nice

The concept of niceness is powerful. When I Googled "nice behavior," what resulted was a list that included "good behavior." That is the inherent problem in understanding niceness—it does not equal goodness. In *The Gift of Fear*, Gavin De Becker (2010) described niceness as a weapon that facilitated offender behavior, characterizing the decision to be nice as a strategic behavior. In reality, nice is a behavior that is a social lubricant. It keeps things pleasant and superficially prosocial. It offers something to the recipient, but ultimately directly benefits the offender. It controls both the victim and the audience to the offense. "I was being better for him than his family, therefore the understanding was is that he owed me," the offender stated, explaining how he was able to control the victim through being nice to him.

Being nice to someone automatically initiates an expectation for the victim's behavior. In general, it is not socially acceptable to respond to niceness with something other than niceness. If a potential victim does not respond as expected to niceness, then that potential victim becomes the problem. A common example I use in my trainings is being offered a drink at a bar. As I am usually alone when I travel, sometimes someone will offer me a drink. There have been times when my refusal has resulted in a negative reaction. One specific incident went something like this: a man and his friends came into the bar where I was eating dinner, celebrating one man's birthday. They were drunk. They offered to buy me a drink, to be included in the celebration. I refused politely. "Oh come on! It's his birthday," they cajoled. I refused politely. Again, they tried to insist I take a drink, saying, "Just one!" For the third time I refused, getting a little annoyed. The bartender then encouraged me to take a drink. After

74 Victim Response to Interpersonal Violence

this exchange, one of the men said, "Hey! Don't be like that!" Obviously, the implication was that I was being a "bitch" and was being a problem. Despite the fact that these men were strangers, the expectation was so strong that I respond to their "niceness" by accepting a drink that the situation became uncomfortable. This pressure to respond to niceness in kind dictates many victim responses and offenders know it.

Nice behavior camouflages offense behavior. Offenders hide their intentions in the guise of doing favors, playing, gift giving, and more. Being nice controls the victim's response because confronting a "nice" person is difficult. The offender can immediately retreat, claiming he was "just being nice" and now the victim is accusing him of something nefarious. If the offender provides many things to the victim, like compliments, attention, or gifts, the victim must lose all those things by reporting abuse or giving up contact with the offender. Remember the power of loss aversion. If the victim is disadvantaged, then the loss of what the offender offers might outweigh the abuse. If the offender is perceived as a "nice person," the victim may make decisions or afford trust to the offender because he does not seem "like that," someone who would hurt her. A parent may place their child in the care of someone nice. The victim, too, might not believe a "nice guy" deserves jail or punishment, while at the same time wishing the abuse would stop. Countless times, I have heard victims of domestic violence say, "I know he is good down deep. I don't want him to go to jail. I love him. I just want it to stop."

Finally, the offender who looks very nice and prosocial may contrast directly with the victim. The victim may have difficulties or symptoms that are not very nice. In a court situation or another situation where the victim's credibility is pitted against the offender, the offender's niceness can have a powerful influence. Take, for example, the stepfather who holds a job, has no criminal record, and goes to church. When his stepdaughter makes allegations of abuse, the stepfather can point out that the stepdaughter lies, runs away, causes trouble at school, and is disrespectful and defiant at home. Regarding the allegations, he can claim, "she has been a handful since I came into this family. She always wanted her parents back together, now she can get her way!" The victim is not very nice—because of the abuse she has been suffering. The offender can use this against her.

Promising to Change: Creating Hope

"All of humanity is based on the notion of what could be, focusing on the future rather than the present," wrote Gurdeep Pandher in his article "The Power of Hope" (2016). Hope is like magic, a powerful belief that "if only" something would happen, a wish will be fulfilled. Hope is cited by psychologists as a critical belief for healing, to motivate change, and to stave off despair. Unfortunately, with offenders, hope becomes another vulnerability.

Victims have many hopes regarding their abuse in their abusers. They want it to stop. They want to be wrong about the abuser. They want the abuser to get help, be sorry, understand the damage they've caused, or have a good explanation for their behavior. "Sometimes she was alone with me and my intentions were to abuse her, sexually assault her, but I didn't, just to get her to trust me, to hope it stopped," an offender explained. Offenders will apologize to the victim, assuring him or her the abuse wasn't deserved, and that they would seek help. Domestic violence offenders are exceptional at creating formulas for the victim to follow in hopes that the assaults will not occur again. "If you could only keep the kids quiet when I get home from work, I won't get so angry," he'll promise. "I wouldn't have to hit you if you would only listen." Alex, another offender, knew his wife would stay with him, because of her hopes and dreams—not only about him, but about herself. "So you know that this person is invested and that they're not going to want to believe the worst because then they question themselves, saying 'what's wrong with me?'"

Offenders can often use therapy, religion, or the threat of consequences to convince the victim to be hopeful. In a study involving the process of recantation of victims of domestic violence, instigating hope of the future together was a consistent part of the offenders dialogue with the victims (Bonomi, Gangamma, Locke, Katafiasz, & Martin, 2011). The offenders in that study made the victims think about their good times together so that the victim's hope for the future gave the motivation to recant allegations of abuse. In our treatment program of violent offenders, we have to be very cautious not to give the victims hope for the offenders' change and make sure that the offenders do not use treatment just to get the victims back. After being confronted by his victim, a family member, one offender promised to go to therapy. While in therapy, he never addressed the sexual abuse of the child, just discussed his "affair" on his wife. However, he told the victim he was addressing his issues in therapy. "I just sat back on her still trusting me to have changed," he stated. "This worked for a little while." The victim eventually found out that he was telling people she was just angry with him because he would not leave his wife for her. She then reported the abuse to officials.

Creating Confusion by Acting Normal

"He would just lay there, asking me about school, like nothing was even happening," the girl explained while describing how her stepfather would call her into his room while he was masturbating openly. "I just tried not look and answer his questions. He would tell me not to be disrespectful, to answer him." The same offender later raped his step-niece. She said

76 Victim Response to Interpersonal Violence

the same thing: "afterwards, he just got up and got dressed. He acted like nothing ever happened. He then asked me if I wanted to go to a different place to hunt. He was like that the whole ride home."

In an informal survey of the offenders in my treatment program, more than 60% of them said that they "acted normal" after an assault, whether it was physical or sexual. They seem to intuitively know that acting as if nothing happened contributed to the victims' disbelief, confusion, and failure to identify the experience as an assault. They knew, too, that this shifted the burden of distress, acting out, or confrontation onto the victim. The victim would have to make an active effort to create conflict. I've seen this technique used over and over again, with offenders who simply got up and invited the victim to breakfast, texted the victim after an assault to talk about what a great time he had, or returned to a party after raping an intoxicated victim to tell his friends how he just got laid. Imagine the position a victim would be in to have to walk into a party and dramatically accuse an offender of raping her when he is acting completely fine. Put yourself in the shoes of a victim who has been beaten by an intimate partner and the risk involved in beginning an argument about what "really happened" last night, while experiencing the relief that the offender is pleasant in the morning. In one of the most disturbing examples I know, the offender brought the victim breakfast in bed, telling her how great she was and explaining that she must have started her period overnight, requiring him to remove all the bloody bedsheets. She was mortified and responded by bringing him new sheets. In fact, he had drugged her and raped her throughout the night, causing her bloody injuries. Although she believed something strange had happened, she could not believe a rapist would bring her breakfast in bed.

"Grooming" or Preparing the Victim to Be a Victim

"Grooming" is a term commonly used by those familiar with sex offenders to describe the process of manipulation, seduction, and introduction to sexual behavior used by the offender to gain the victim's compliance and reduce the victim's willingness to disclose. Grooming behavior encompasses the behaviors described above, like forming attachment or gaining the victim's cooperation, as well as desensitizing the victim to sexual or abusive behaviors. Offenders do this with victims who are close to them physically as well as those who are not; for instance, over the internet.

Whether it is physical abuse or sexual abuse, offenders who want to maintain ongoing access to their victims will not typically engage in abrupt, overt acts of violence suddenly and early in their relationship with the victim. This type of assault is more easily defined by the victim as abuse and is likely to rupture the relationship. Instead, offenders will cross boundaries over time, introducing new acts as they test the

"Influence of the Offender" 77

victims' compliance and alliance with them. Violent offenders will begin violence by grabbing, pushing, restraining, or blocking the exit of the victim. At each escalation, the victim accommodates to the acts, growing desensitized and blaming herself for "making him mad" or "allowing" the behavior. As one sexual offender of children described it:

> It started out with getting them in my room, my bedroom, laying on the bed playing video games because kids like video games. Video-games is a big thing that I use because it's convenient. It's there on my bed. Then I would wrestle with them, a lot of horseplay. Young boys love to horse play so I used that to my advantage and I get aroused by wrestling and with them in the bed. To get them to feel safe or secure with me assaulting them, we would wrestle and I'd say, "it's getting hot in here," then I would take my shirt off. Most of the time they'd follow cue and take their shirt off or I'd take their shirt off. A lot of time went in until it got to the point where I was actu-ally naked, lying in bed with my victims, getting their clothes off. It took a lot. Over time it happened, it wasn't right away. One thing at a time, it started as wrestling to taking their clothes off, wrestling in bed, until I was until the point where I was manipulating the victims into letting me orally assault them.

Not only is this process insidious, it incorporates the concept of victim cooperation. Additionally, most of the offense behavior that is stimulat-ing for the offender is innocuous to the victim. The victim has no idea that they are in a process that is leading to their assault. The victim would only be able to identify a small portion of the offender's offense behavior, while the offender was getting sexual gratification throughout the entire process—even the nonsexual behavior, like wrestling.

Offenders engage in post-offense behavior to continue the grooming process. The offender may compliment or cuddle with the victim they have just sexually assaulted. The violent offender might apologize, send flowers, or be extra sweet to the victim. Post-offense grooming can be as important as pre-offense grooming to ensure that the victim remains conflicted about disclosing. Joe, an offender of boys, described this:

> Every time I've offended I always tried to make it as peaceful and non-violent as possible. Kind of in my head I'm thinking don't scare him or traumatize him or anything because then when they go home—I make it like a fun thing, so that when I'm done victimizing, I kid around with them or joke with them, so by the time they get home they're in a good mood again.

The offender is always focused on succeeding in their crime.

Past Experience With the Offender

"He would stand there in front of me and say, 'I will not be denied' and put his crotch in my face," my client explained. "I knew if I did not suck him off, there would be hell to pay." Experience with the offender is likely to have taught the victim a great deal about the offender's reaction and the best way to respond to the offender. As in the case above, what might look like consensual submission to a sexual act was actually a strategic decision to avoid abuse. A victim could have learned the offender is always calm, contrite, or kind after an assault—escape is unnecessary. Some victims of domestic violence might even provoke the offender to "get it over with," then go on with a more pleasant night instead of waiting in terror to be abused. He might go to sleep after a beating or sexual assault. Victims use their knowledge of an offender, current or past, to guide their decision-making in response to the offender's behavior. A victim who has learned that resistance is futile might submit. Another victim might have learned to "pretend normal" in order not to provoke further abuse from the offender.

Some of these decisions might seem superficially bizarre. For example, in one case, a 14-year old victim was sexually assaulted by her stepfather after he murdered her mother. In fact, he assaulted her while her mother lay dying next to her in the same bed. The victim got up, went to the living room with the offender, and watched a movie with him. She did not call for help. However, throughout the movie, she got up intermittently, got her siblings some clothing and gathered their medication, picked up some things, and persistently and calmly talked to her stepfather about getting help. Not only was she in shock, but she was keeping him calm and herself safe. It is critical to ask the victim about how they made the decisions they did and what they knew about the offender that guided those decisions.

A victim does not have to be previously victimized directly by that offender to have the experience with the offender guide their decisions. A child who has witnessed their father be violent to their mother can be more vulnerable to complying with sexual abuse from that offender, having witnessed his capacity for violence (Bancroft, Silverman, & Ritchie, 2012). In some of my cases with the military, the victim's knowledge of the offender's proficiency with weapons was a factor in decision-making in relation to the offender.

The offenders themselves use the victims' experiences against the victims as well. The offender might tell the victim "you know how I get," as a warning and way to blame the victim. The abuser could refer to a past sexual assault to convince the victim of her compliance, saying something like, "you let me do it last time, now you're saying no?" The intimacy in relationships gives offenders information about their victims that can be utilized effectively to harm the victim by provoking her, shaming her, making her feel guilty, or confusing her. "You see rape everywhere, I think you're getting confused," one coercive partner said to his victim, referring to her history of assault. "You are so oversensitive." Other offenders freely admit to coercing their partners through knowledge of their past sexual history. One man said, "yeah, so what, I told her she slept with some black guy in the past, she should be happy I will have sex with her." In fact, past experience with the offender can be used by others to blame the victim as well, like past consensual contacts, agreements for "rough sex," or permission for anal penetration. For both the offender and the audience, it can be as if once consent has been given, it can never be revoked.

Influence of the Offender on the Community

There is an element to all offender assaults that is generally ignored, and that is the audience to the assault. By audience I mean the community of the offender and victim, including the judge, jury, panel, or even those of us involved in the investigation and prosecution. If the offender is effective at manipulating the perceptions and thinking of the audience, he can get away with offense by producing disbelief, confusion, or doubt about the victim, even in cases with the strongest evidence. If an offender can convincingly assert that his wife is crazy or vindictive, then her reports that he has battered her or abused their children can be dismissed. If an offender can present a persona that proves they are "not like that," allegations of rape or child abuse can go unbelieved. Given this, the offender's manipulation and grooming of the community is just as important as the offender's influence on the victim.

Offenders may walk into the criminal justice system with a leg up on success already, simply by their status or how they look. According to a study by Gunnell and Ceci (2010), attractive and emotional defendants were more likely to be believed and less likely to be convicted than unattractive defendants. Jurors were influenced by "extralegal" factors regarding the offender and victim, like victim behavior and emotionality, despite the evidence. In appealing to emotional reasoning versus rational thinking, offenders can distract jurors from facts, as well as perpetuate reliance on nonrational thinking and knowledge. This study might provide some insight on how offenders activate disbelief by garnering trust and attachment, by acting nice, and by presenting as prosocial to others. It also speaks to some of the lingering assessments of assault that rely on emotional thinking, like "she pushed his buttons," "she's too fat to rape," or "he seems okay, it didn't kill him, so it wasn't that bad." Status is another powerful influence, as we have seen in high-profile cases.

80 Victim Response to Interpersonal Violence

In talking to many people, I have found that high-status offenders are afforded innocence through a variety of ways: "they can get laid anytime they want," victims are "gold diggers" out for attention or money, or the offender's status in and of itself makes the offender a target. Any review of articles and comments about high-profile accused and accusers will reveal this.

Creating the Public Persona

Most of us have people in their lives that we believe we know well. We judge him or her on how that person presents to us, without acknowledging that people live private lives where they show parts of themselves that are intimate, sexual, and secret. This is sometimes called the "double life" of the offender (Salter, 2003). Offenders rely on status, position, and convincing others that they are incapable of offending. They put effort into their public persona so that when allegations arise, the victim is disbelieved.

How are they so successful at this? It is apparent they are, as die-hard supporters of convicted offenders like Bill Cosby demonstrated. Even after conviction, some are convinced of his innocence, citing his television character, charitable works, or public personality as proof of his innocence. When asked how they foster this type of allegiance in others, offenders are quick to explain this to me. "I think I did the same thing with the parents, I groomed them as well," said a convicted priest who abused boys. "I would visit the house, by making myself available to them, make it look like I was taking care of their son and helping him in various ways, so not only did I groomed my victim, I groomed their parents." Another, who was assaulting an adult woman and had assaulted a child, stated, "if there was something going on, or someone needed something, I would help out. That was the biggest thing I hid behind. The same thing at work, I would be overly, overly helpful to keep them off track." He conveyed his preemptive planning too, saying, "so if anything were to ever come out, I could use that too. I would also be able to use the same thing, like, 'Oh come on, you guys know me. You trust me with this, you trust me with that—there's no way I would do anything like that.'"

This offender highlights how to use other's egocentric needs against them. We all believe we are good judges of character, so when we are betrayed, we seek solace. Some of that solace can come from denial that the offender supports. It is easier to disbelieve an allegation than to believe that someone we care for or have invested in is a perpetrator. "They believed the best about me and she would not want to believe that she had been betrayed or been tricked. Putting myself in her shoes now, I would feel dumb, that's how I would feel," relayed an offender who had a wife, children, and a high-status job. He went on to say, "I wore the white hat in a lot of different roles. I had the role of being a prosecutor which comes with certain trust, public trust, trust of the coworkers. I was in charge of putting bad guys away, so no one looks at you like you're the bad guy." An offending priest stated, "I knew he didn't think anyone would believe him, because of my position—I always hid behind that, my position, I knew no one would think I was capable of that." Offenders are highly aware of their status in the community, as well as others' investment in believing in them, fostering it to their advantage.

Controlling the Information

Offenders understand that another powerful way to control and groom the environment is to control the information available. Offenders may tell on themselves; for example, going to their commander when they fear allegations, to explain that they're going through a difficult divorce because of an affair, telling the commander to expect rumors to go around. They offer plausible explanations and justifications for allegations, showing their friend the sexting they did with their victims before the assault. One offender, who was abusing his four-year-old daughter, would go out drinking with his friends, lamenting about how his wife did not want to have sex with him and didn't love him anymore, far before he was caught abusing the child. "Yeah, it worked with people—it worked with a lot of people, so much so that when I came out on parole and sat down with them to say yeah, this is really what happened, they still didn't want to believe it," said a convicted rapist of a child and adult victim. "I've had to cut ties with a lot of people who didn't want to let go of the lie that I built up so great."

Creating a Victim's Reputation and Setting Up Retaliation

In controlling the information and exploiting victim vulnerabilities, offenders can create a perception of the victim that diminishes the victim's credibility and increases the likelihood that the offender will get away with offending. The more the offender can portray the victim as problematic in any way, the less likely it is that the victim will be believed, especially if the offender has been successful at creating a nice persona. Domestic violence offenders are notorious for appearing calm and collected when police respond to a domestic situation, while the victim is angry, hysterical, and terrified that the police have appeared. In custody court, when a custody evaluation is ordered, the victim might feel the need to urgently convince the evaluator that her partner has been dangerous in order to protect the children. The normal-sounding, calm, and prosocial ex-husband who expresses sincere concern over his ex-wife's mental health can fool

82 Victim Response to Interpersonal Violence

the examiner, causing a conclusion that the excitable wife is overly dramatic and focused only on disparaging her ex-husband with allegations of abuse. "The lies that I was spreading, saying she's the reason why my wife and I split up. It was an affair, she was upset I wasn't leaving my wife. It was the multiple lies," the rapist stated, explaining why the victim eventually went to the police. Another portrayed his teenage victim as an overly sexualized child who attempted to seduce him on multiple occasions, walking out of the shower without a towel or flirting with him. His friends showed up at his sentencing hearing, after he murdered the child's mother and raped the child again, to talk about how the child manipulated him sexually.

This portrayal of the victim can also ready the supporters of the offender to retaliate. If others truly believe that the victim is maligning the offender with false allegations, retaliation can soon follow. Retaliation can include influencing the victim's children, antagonizing the victim at work, or tormenting the victim over social media. Retaliation can include taking the side of the offender, writing letters in support of the offender and against the victim, or ostracizing the victim in a closed community like the military. Child victims can be retaliated against by their siblings for ruining the family, rejected by extended family, or pressured to recant. An investigator or prosecutor must monitor these issues to offer support to the victim and prevent the victim's withdrawal from prosecution.

Deception After the Disclosure

Offenders put a significant amount of energy into convincing others that the victim is lying if and when the disclosure is made. Interestingly, although the victim is hesitant to disclose, hates talking about the abuse, and fears disbelief, the offender often is active in defending himself, garnering support, offering alternative explanations for the abuse, and exploiting and enhancing the confusion in disbelief of the people and their environment. Many offenders I have treated have presented letters of reference or recommendation from others in their community who are willing to write about the offender's intention, character, and capacity for the offense. "He's 'not like that,' 'you don't know him the way we know him,' I went to the judge with a stack of letters," an offender explained. This offender was caught with hundreds and hundreds of illegal images of child sexual abuse—despite this, his supporters wrote these letters, citing that he only made a mistake.

Offenders perpetuate their denial by citing the victim's motive for retaliation. It is true that victims' disclosures may be triggered by a significant event, like a divorce, being punished by or betrayed by the offender, or another rupture in the relationship with the offender that affords the victim the distance or empowerment to make a disclosure. The offenders then use this to their advantage, saying that the ex-wife is vindictive and just wants the kids, that the child is angry at punishment so is making up a disclosure, or that the victim is retaliating for some other betrayal. "What triggered her was that it came back to her the lies that I was spreading," the offender explained. He had assaulted the victim through her childhood, then again when she was an older adolescent. "She found out I was telling people that she was just angry at me for not leaving my wife, that we were having an affair," he said. Another offender convinced a victim's mother that she was lying. "When she first told her mother, I convinced her mother, 'no she's lying,'" he said, "She got grounded 'cause she did something stupid and now she's mad at me, that's why she said it." In fact, this was true. The victim did disclose because the perpetrator grounded her; however, he had been sexually assaulting her for months. A third example was from an offender who later murdered the victim's mother, along with three other people. The victim, the eight-year-old girl the offender was watching, disclosed that he had sexually assaulted her while her mother was gone. The mother initially believed the child, gathering evidence to report to police immediately. However, the next day, the offender persuaded her to go on a three-day "honeymoon," on which he lavished her with compliments and sex, using his sexual interest in the mother to convince her he was not attracted to children.

As in the previous example, offenders will rely on ignorance, misinformation, and seemingly reasonable assertions to confuse people. For example, one offender asked, "When would I have time to do that? I work 12, 14, 16 hours a day. What you think I'm doing, sneaking around at night?" Again, that was exactly what he was a doing, to abuse the children while they slept. "If I had planned that, wouldn't I have locked the front door?" another offender asked his wife, who had caught him assaulting their child, in order to make his acts look like an accident. Offenders use our ignorance of deviance, our wish to deny sexual assault, our biases, the behavior of the victim, and what seems like legitimate issues to create confusion and cultivate our disbelief in the victims.

Summary

Offender influence on the victim is significant, but often ignored. Part of this might be explained by the fact that the offender's behavior cannot typically be introduced during trial. When grooming, manipulation, or other issues are brought into play by prosecutors, the objection is often that the prosecutor is attempting to profile the defendant by explaining offender behavior. However, when the offender behavior is framed as a factor that dictates or influences victim response or victim dynamics, that offender's behavior can be introduced. For example, "what did he do to keep you from telling?" is a question that can be easily defended when a victim's delay of disclosure is an issue at hand. A good investigation or interview by the prosecutor can reveal all of the victim's responses in the context of the offender's behavior.

Remember, offenders control victims and very concrete and identifiable ways, like controlling finances or engaging in threats. However, there are more subtle and insidious ways that the offender can influence the victim and guide their responses, including:

- Getting the victim's cooperation;
- Exploiting the victim's vulnerabilities;
- Getting the victim to love them and have hopes with them through building attachment;
- Using niceness to control the victim and manage the perceptions and the environment;
- Grooming the victim;
- Creating a public persona that supports the community's denial of the allegations; and
- Controlling information.

Insightful questions about the offender's ability to manipulate and control the victim not only reveal the offender but also support the victim's growing understanding about how he or she was preyed upon. This understanding and insight can facilitate a shift in the victim's view of the perpetrator and of him- or herself. It can also plant seeds for the victims to change their interpretation of the offender's nice behavior so that their guilt and ambivalence about reporting is mitigated.

References

Amnesty International. (1975). *Report on Torture*. London: Duckworth Press.

Bancroft, L., Silverman, J., & Ritchie, D. (2012). *The batterer as parent: Addressing the impact of domestic violence on family dynamics*. Los Angeles, CA: Sage.

Bonomi, A. E., Gangamma, R., Locke, C. R., Katafiasz, H., & Martin, D. (2011). "Meet me at the hill where we used to park": Interpersonal processes associated with victim recantation. *Social Science & Medicine, 73*, 1054–1061.

de Becker, G. (2010). *The gift of fear*. New York: Dell.

Gunnell, J., & Ceci, S. (2010). When emotionality trumps reason: A study of individual processing style and juror bias. *Behavioral Sciences & the Law, 28*, 850–877. doi:10.1002/bsl.939

Katz, C., & Barnetz, Z. (2016). Children's narratives of alleged child sexual abuse offender behavior and the manipulation process. *Psychology of Violence, 6*(2), 223–232. doi:10.1037/a0039023

Pandher, G. (2016, May 17). The power of hope. *Life*. Retrieved from www.huffpost.com/entry/the-power-of-hope_b_10007390

Salter, A. (2003). *Predators, pedophiles, rapists, and other sex offenders: Who they are, how they operate, and how we can protect ourselves and our children*. New York: Basic Books.

Chapter 5

"I Should Have Kicked His Ass"

Male Victims of Intimate Violence

They were thrilled to be there. They both married and they both have children, so it didn't kill them.
—Barbra Streisand, quoted in Variety *about the alleged victims of Michael Jackson (Saperstein, 2019, March 22)*

"Male rape emerging as one of the most underreported weapons of war" was a recent headline on the Fox News website (McKay, 2019, March 21). The deleterious impact of rape has always been understood and used as a weapon in wartime. However, the reasons for and impact of rape of men and boys during wartime can have different social, cultural, and psychological effects on the victims. In cultures in which homosexuality is outlawed, male victims of sex crimes can be arrested. The rape of men and boys is often more physically violent to the victims. Men continue to vastly underreport the crime.

Most research has been done on female victims of sexual assault. In fact, in most of the sexual assault or domestic violence cases I have worked on had a male perpetrator and a female victim. I have worked with many male victims of sexual assault, abused both by women and men, older girls and boys. With the exception of the child victims I have worked with, not one of the adult male victims seeking therapy has ever been part of a formal prosecutorial process. And of the thousands of sexual offender evaluations I have performed, only a small number have included an adult perpetrator and an adult male victim. In these cases, all of the perpetrators have been male. My program has never once received a referral for the treatment of a domestic violence abuser who assaulted his adult male partner, even though these exist.

Male victims face many internal and external hurdles to overcome regarding help-seeking, reporting, and prosecution of sexual assault. Many of the factors described in the previous chapters can be applied to male victims. However, this chapter attempts to address some factors or issues unique to men in our society that contribute to vast underreporting and under-prosecution of the sexual or intimate partner abuse of men. This book is not meant to be a comprehensive book on all the issues faced by victims of intimate violence. However, in addressing the abuse of male victims, law enforcement and prosecutors need to be aware of unique issues faced by male victims in order to improve our response to these victims, as well as successfully investigate and prosecute cases involving them. This chapter provides a very brief overview of some of the issues facing male victims that investigators and prosecutors should consider.

It is commonly accepted that about one in six adult males have been sexually assaulted. Statistics about male sexual assault vary, as it is generally believed that male sexual assault is severely underreported. Additionally, traditional research has not captured male sexual assault due to definitions of penetrative acts. There have been surprising findings from recent crime victimization studies regarding male victims. In 2013, the National Crime Victimization Survey showed that 38% of the sexual violence reported was against male victims (Stemple & Meyer, 2014). The researchers concluded that problematic legal definitions of rape and assault, as well as traditional gender stereotypes, contributed to the underreporting. A recent report of sexual assault in the military estimated that 7,500 men were sexually assaulted in 2018; 43% of these reported having been assaulted by a woman (Department of Defense, 2019). Only 17% of these victims reported their sexual assault. Additionally, few studies or surveys incorporate the inclusion of inmates, a population fraught with the sexual assault of men (Stemple & Meyer, 2014). Tewksbury (2007) concludes, "men who are sexually assaulted are highly unlikely to report their victimization or to seek medical or mental health services (p. 31)." Studies continue to support this conclusion a decade later (Lowe & Rogers, 2017; Donne et al., 2018).

Being a male victim in the gendered arena of sexual assault and intimate partner violence is difficult. There are some basic facts that can segregate a male victim. Most victims are female. Most perpetrators are male. The male victim can be isolated from peers, other victims, and helpers. The myth that male victims will automatically become perpetrators makes these victims fearful. Small boys have asked me if they are going to become like the men who assaulted them, in part thanks to adult perpetrators who blame their own abuse for their choice to rape.

"Be a Man:" Traditional Masculinity and Societal Messages

Traditional masculinity promotes the idea that to be a man, a man must be strong, dominant, and invulnerable. It embodies a constellation of standards and expectations that reject femininity, vulnerability, and weakness, while promoting achievement, emotional hardness, and violence. It contributes to the belief that men are unlikely victims of sexual assault or battering. Rigid adherence to or socialization to traditional masculine roles and expectations has been found to produce emotional and psychological dysfunction in boys and men, so much so that the American Psychological Association (APA) issued new guidelines on the treatment of men and boys in 2018 so that treatment professionals hold specific awareness of the social and cultural stereotypes and biases associated with masculinity (APA, 2018). These guidelines acknowledge that socialization to masculinity impacts a male's relationships with others, especially other men; impacts help-seeking; and promotes violence, suicide, and risk-taking behaviors. Men have higher death rates than women related to this socialization, because of their involvement with risk-taking and violence. Colloquially, socialization to manhood to a detrimental degree is referred to as "toxic masculinity."

Not only is risk-taking increased, help-seeking or self-care behaviors are also less common in men (APA, 2018) for all sorts of health issues. These issues are compounded by the shame, vulnerability, and stigma of sexual assault or battering, making men even less likely to seek help for the assault. Riccardi (2010) wrote about a small number of male veterans who were victims of assault. All stated that the loss of their "manliness" was their biggest problem. A male victim I evaluated who had been raped by a group of men after leaving his ship had chronic feelings of inadequacy and vulnerability following his assault. "I can't leave the house. For the first time in my life, I found out I couldn't protect myself," he said. "Me. Tough guy. Never walked away from anything. Now I am just a big pussy." Study after study of male victims cite the socialization of masculinity and cultural norms, acceptance of rape myths regarding male rape, and minimization of the assaults of men as barriers to male reporting and help-seeking (Artime, McCallum, & Peterson, 2014; Davies, 2002).

Having a Penis

"It was easy, easy to convince them and myself really that I wasn't hurting anybody," he said, explaining his abuse of boys to me. "I mean, they would enjoy it. It felt good. They would get hard." The physiological response of an erection can be very confusing to male victims. As children, we are taught that sexual abuse is "bad touch," but the sensation that perpetrators can produce in their male victims counters that teaching. Offenders who abuse children—both male and female offenders—can use the male sexual response as "proof" to themselves and the victim that the victim "likes" the abuse, is actively participating in the abuse, and is consenting to the assault.

Male sexual response is used as reinforcement for many harmful ideas about male sexuality. Although perpetrators camouflage sexual assault in the guise of unmanageable male sexual arousal and the idea that "boys will be boys," male victims have to make sense of the disparity between their emotional and psychological response and their physical one. "I mean, it's not like he was really hurting me, and I went back. I let him do it some more," an adult male told me, trying to explain his confusion at age 53 about still blaming himself for his assaults by an adult when he was young. "There is no such thing as a bad blow job," a psychologist flippantly stated to me regarding the treatment of male victims. This shocking and disheartening statement from a professional clearly revealed the belief that men will always be up for and grateful for sex. Loss of control of your body is one of the profound psychological impacts of rape. Imagine if that loss came from a sense that your own body betrayed you, something male victims can experience.

The idea that men are sexually insatiable contributes to the persistent idea that male sexual assault is not as bad as female sexual assault. This is especially true when it comes to men being raped by women, whether as boys or adults (Stemple & Meyer, 2014). Men who are assaulted by women face double the disbelief—not only are men not victims, but women are not perpetrators (Davies, 2002). Male rape myths contribute to minimizing male sexual assault (Davies, Gilston, & Rogers, 2012; Stemple & Meyer, 2014). It can also contribute to further shame when a male victim experiences sexual dysfunction following an assault (Tewksbury, 2007). Sexual dysfunction is a serious issue for male victims, who then can struggle not feeling manly, question their sexuality, or have significant intimacy issues.

The legal issue of penetration can be problematic for male victims of assault. Statutes typically define rape as requiring penetration of the vulva or another orifice. What happens in the case of a male victim when the perpetrator *uses the victim's penis for penetration?* If a man is sleeping or intoxicated and a female perpetrator stimulates him to the point that she can penetrate herself with his penis, this could become legally confusing. McKeever (2018) argues for changes in the legal definitions of rape and the requirement for penetration because of this. She points out that the law generally reflects two notions: that it is worse to forcibly penetrate someone than to force someone to penetrate you and that sex is something that men do to women. Addressing the issue of penetration, especially in cases when the male victim is not anally penetrated, is important, especially considering that recent statistics suggest that a large percentage of men and boys report female perpetrators (Stemple & Meyer, 2014).

In fact, issues of physiological response and the accepted narrative of rape leads to men failing to acknowledge their experiences as rape or assault. When the perpetrator did not use force or was not male, men did not accurately label their assaults. Only 24% of men who were raped in one study acknowledged the rape (Artime et al., 2014). As with female victims, when a man does not acknowledge the assault, he does not seek help or understand the impact of the assault on him. Additionally, a history of victimization contributes significantly to the risk of revictimization in men (Artime et al., 2014; Tewksbury, 2007).

Shame and Stigma

Most victims feel some sort of shame, but shame is the most common emotional experience of male victims of assault (Tewksbury, 2007). Shame was one of the biggest barriers to help-seeking in a study of college students (Sable, Danis, Mauzy, & Gallagher, 2006). The sources of shame come from the experience of weakness and vulnerability; the failure to "be a man;" the loss of control; and, possibly, the physiological response of the victim. Men are more likely to label themselves as a victim of assault when assaulted by a man, perhaps because abuse by a woman is superficially less shameful as it is less challenging to masculinity (Artime et al., 2014). Lowe and Rogers (2017) reviewed many sources of shame and stigma faced by male victims, including homophobia, masculine self-identity, generalized vulnerability, fear of ridicule, and feelings of isolation. Shame and stigma were greater barriers to men versus women because of these issues (Sable et al., 2006).

Shame, fear of blame, and stigma are contributors to social isolation. As social support has a profoundly positive or negative impact on victim outcomes and help-seeking, fear of stigma and shame can keep men from the very thing that could be helpful. However, when reporting, male victims report having a poor experience with law enforcement (Walker, Archer, & Davies, 2005). Other male victims in a very small sample reported being disbelieved by their male psychiatrist, being unwilling to report the assault, or being diagnosed with malingering because of the symptoms of trauma (Riccardi, 2010).

As men experience the aftereffects of assault, like substance abuse, trauma-related symptoms, or depression, the symptoms can lead to shame. As discussed, men are less likely to acknowledge and seek help for emotional or psychological issues (APA, 2018). Hostility, self-harm, and withdrawal are common (Tewksbury, 2007), likely leading to more shame, not only for the symptoms the victim is having, but for the way he is acting and alienating others.

Victim Blaming

Shame and stigma are not unexpected feelings for male victims, especially when confronted by the rape myths about men and the victim blaming that occurs. Male victims face a different type of victim blaming than female victims. Women might be expected to resist; however, male victims are expected to have prevented their own victimization. Studies show that men are more likely to blame other men for being victims because of their lack of successful resistance against another man (Davies et al., 2012; Davies, Rogers, & Bates, 2008).

Male victims fear disbelief, blame, or judgement by male helpers (Riccardi, 2010) and law enforcement (Hammond, Ioannou, & Fewster, 2016; NCAVP, 2010). Although female victims face the same fears, men believe that they should have been able to fend off the attack, will be arrested as a perpetrator, or will be dismissed because they "wanted it" or were lucky to be having sex. Men are more likely, too, to be blamed for having initiated the sexual contact, for being sexually interested in the assault, or for being the actual perpetrator. One victim of sadistic abuse by his girlfriend sought police help after being hit with a frying pan (skull fracture), bitten (70 bite marks), and having his fingers and penis cut with scissors. He escaped from the home 70 pounds lighter than he was three months prior. When he sought help, the police did not believe his initial account of the abuse, denying that "just a woman" could have hurt him without him defending himself. It was only when he "admitted" to being gang raped by three other men did police take him more seriously.

Sexual or gender orientation can complicate issues faced generally by male victims. Gay, bisexual, and transgender persons are more at risk for sexual violence than others (NCAVP, 2010). These victims face having their sexual assaults by other men minimized. Just a few months ago, in a training for attorneys, an attorney opined that if a man raped a gay man, it wouldn't be as traumatizing because the victim was "used to it." When I questioned this, saying by that logic, a heterosexual, sexually active woman shouldn't be traumatized by being raped by a man, the lawyer looked perplexed. Gender- and sexual-minority clients continue to fear prejudice, homophobia, or ignorance when help-seeking or reporting to law enforcement (Donne et al., 2018). Given that law enforcement is a male-dominated profession and males judge males more harshly, the added component of being a sexual minority could be daunting.

Minimization of Assault

There is the significant persistent problem that male sexual assault is perceived as less severe than female sexual assault. Not only do the victims themselves fail to identify their victimization, others do as well. Research has repeatedly demonstrated that subjects in studies involving the sexual assault of males minimized the severity of the assaults (Davies et al., 2008; Davies et al., 2012).

In fact, for male victims of rape, injury is far more likely. The injuries came from the use of physical force on the victims, as well as forcible anal penetration (Walker et al., 2005; Tewksbury, 2007). Physical injury is related to immediate help-seeking in male victims; however, they tend to only seek treatment for the injuries and not the assault. Typically, in cases of injury, men are raped by other men. However, men are sexually assaulted by women as well, without injury.

Access to Services

Although all assault victims face limitations in access to services for a variety of reasons, male adult victims face specific issues. Studies have shown that male victims can be specifically excluded from the services of rape crisis centers or hotlines (Tewksbury, 2007), that sexual assault examiners are not routinely taught about examination of male victims (Davies, 2002), and, in general there are few resources available (Walker et al., 2005). This has not significantly changed (Lowe & Rogers, 2017). There are typically limited or no resources for male victims of intimate partner violence (National Domestic Violence Hotline, 2019; Stiles, Ortiz, & Keene, 2017; Vernon, 2017). Many rape or domestic violence centers are staffed by women, who might have been victims themselves and may have difficulty serving male clients. Even in my own practice, victim services for men have been hampered by men's unwillingness to be part of group treatment as a victim or deal with the experience of their abuse. Most of the men willing to address their victimization have been clients treated for offending, who then reveal their victimization. The only two male victim participants in one study who sought treatment had negative experiences (Donne et al., 2018).

Summary

Male victims of interpersonal violence underreport sexual assault and underutilize the criminal justice system much more than female victims. They fail to acknowledge their own victimization and need for help. Though they experience the same issues and barriers to help-seeking as all victims do, men face some unique challenges that present even more complex hurdles to overcome to seek help and prosecution. These include:

- Socialization regarding masculinity, stereotypes, and biases;
- The strength of the shame and stigma male victims feel;
- Unique physiological and legal issues related to erections and penetration;
- Victim blaming and minimization of the assaults based on expectations of strength and sexual interests;
- Fear of judgement, shame, and stigma of being a male victim; and
- Limited resources for male victims, real and perceived.

Male victims of sexual violence have a significant rate of revictimization. Male victims also suffer significant psychological effects of assault, like

92 Victim Response to Interpersonal Violence

risk-taking, self-harm, depression, sexual dysfunction, and suicidality. Their unwillingness or inability to get help for these issues, as well as their unwillingness to seek legal recourse against their abusers, pose even greater challenges for investigators and prosecutors who seek justice for all victims of violence. Training, awareness, and confrontation of the stereotypes and biases male victims face are imperative to facilitate the participation of male victims in the prosecutorial process.

References

American Psychological Association. (2018). *Guidelines for psychological practice with boys and men.* Retrieved from www.apa.org/about/policy/boys-men-practice-guidelines.pdf

Artime, T., McCallum, E., & Peterson, Z. (2014). Men's acknowledgement of their sexual victimization experiences. *Psychology of Men & Masculinity, 15*(3), 313–323. doi:10.1037/a0033376

Davies, M. (2002). Male sexual assault victims: A selective review of the literature and implications for support services. *Aggression and Violent Behavior, 7,* 203–214.

Davies, M., Gilston, J., & Rogers, P. (2012). Examining the relationships between male rape myth acceptance, female rape myth acceptance, victim blame, homophobia, gender roles, and ambivalent sexism. *Journal of Interpersonal Violence, 27*(14), 2807–2823. doi:10.1177/0886260512438281

Davies, M., Rogers, P., & Bates, J. (2008). Blame toward male rape victims in a hypothetical sexual assault as a function victim sexuality and degree of resistance. *Journal of Homosexuality, 55*(3), 533–544. doi:10.1080/00918360802345339

Department of Defense. (2019, April 9). *Annual report on sexual assault in the military fiscal year 2018.* Retrieved from www.sapr.mil/sites/default/files/DoD_Annual_Report_on_Sexual_Assault_in_the_Military.pdf

Donne, M., DeLuca, J., Pleskach, P., Bromson, C., Mosley, M., Perez, E., . . . Frye, V. (2018). Barriers to and facilitators of help-seeking behavior among men who experience sexual violence. *American Journal of Men's Health, 12*(2), 189–201. doi:10.1177/1557988317740665

Hammond, L., Ionannou, M., & Fewster, M. (2016). Perceptions of male rape and sexual assault in a male sample from the United Kingdom: Barriers to reporting and the impacts of victimization. *Journal of Investigative Psychology and Offender Profiling, 14,* 133–149. doi:10.1002/jip.1462

Lowe, M., & Rogers, P. (2017). The scope of male rape: A selective review of research, policy and practice. *Aggression and Violent Behavior, 35,* 38–43. doi:10.1016/j.avb.2017.06.007

McKay, H. (2019, March 21). *Male rape emerges as one of the most underreported weapons of war.* Retrieved from www.foxnews.com/world/male-rape-emerging-as-one-of-the-most-underreported-weapons-of-todays-wars

McKeever, N. (2018). Can a woman rape a man and why does it matter? *Criminal Law and Philosophy, 1*–21. Retrieved from https://link.springer.com/article/10.1007/s11572-018-9485-6

"Male Victims of Intimate Violence" 93

National Domestic Violence Hotline. (2019). *Who will help me? Domestic violence survivors speak out about law enforcement responses.* Washington, DC. Retrieved from www.thehotline.org/resources/law-enforcement-responses

NCAVP. (2010). *Hate violence against the LGBTQ communities in the U.S. in 2009.* Retrieved from https://avp.org/wp-content/uploads/2017/04/2011_NCAVP_HV_Reports.pdf

Riccardi, P. (2010). Male rape: The silent victim and gender of the listener. *The Primary Care Companion to the Journal of Clinical Psychiatry, 12*(6). doi:10.4088/PCC.10I00993whi

Sable, M., Danis, F., Mauzy, D., & Gallagher, S. (2006). Barriers to reporting sexual assault for women and men: Perspectives of college students. *Journal of American College Health, 55*, 157–162.

Saperstein, P. (2019, March 22). *Barbra Streisand believes the Michael Jackson accusers, but says "They were thrilled to be there".* Retrieved from https://variety.com/2019/music/news/barbra-streisand-michael-jackson-accusers-thrilled-1203170747/

Stemple, L., & Meyer, I. (2014). The sexual victimization of men in America: New data challenge old assumptions. *American Journal of Public Health, 104*(6), 19–27.

Stiles, E., Ortiz, I., & Keene, J. (2017). Serving male-identified survivors of intimate partner violence. *National Resource Center on Domestic Violence.* Retrieved from https://vawnet.org/sites/default/files/assets/files/2017–07/NRCDV_TAG-ServingMaleSurvivors-July2017.pdf

Tewksbury, R. (2007). Effects of sexual assaults on men: Physical, mental, and sexual consequences. *International Journal of Men's Health, 6*(1), 22–35. doi:10.3149/jmh.0601.22

Vernon, D. (2017). Has society created social injustice for male victims of domestic violence? *Undergraduate Honors Capstone Projects, 227.* Retrieved from https://digitalcommons.usu.edu/honors/227

Walker, J., Archer, J., & Davies, M. (2005). Effects of rape on men: A descriptive analysis. *Archives of Sexual Behavior, 34*(1), 69–80. doi:10.1007/s10508-005-1001-0

Section 2

Common Types of Victim Responses

Chapter 6

"What Was I Supposed to Say?"

Issues in Disclosures of Assault

What was I supposed to say? Who was I going to tell? What good would it do anyway? I wasn't ready to do anything about it. I didn't even know how bad it was until I started seeing you and talking about it. To this day I still can't remember all of. It comes and goes.
—Victim of domestic abuse

WHY? WHY? *Why isn't he in trouble?* WHY DOESN'T HE HAVE TO TELL PEOPLE WHAT HE DID TO ME? *Why am I the one in trouble? Why do I have to talk about it?*
—10-year-old victim of abuse

"Do you see all these lies? I mean, first she acts like nothing at all happened! Then she tells one investigator it was on the 29th—that was a Monday! Not on a weekend like she told someone else," the defense attorney argued. Disclosures of victims, if they happen at all, are scrutinized extensively in the criminal justice process. When, how, and to whom disclosures are made are examined, used as evidence against the victim, and understood in the context of misinformation and misunderstanding of the process of disclosure, the impact of trauma on disclosure, and in forgetting common sense issues of memory altogether.

There seems to be the expectation for victims that if something terrible happens, like sexual or physical assault, a victim will immediately report, clearly remember, and have no difficulty disclosing that assault. The criminal justice system has impossible standards for human memory under the best of circumstances, never mind in the context of trauma, confusion, and betrayal. Crimes of intimate violence often demand compliance to these impossible standards because of the private nature of the assault. Because there are typically no witnesses to intimate partner or sexual assaults, a victim's disclosure and memory of the assault are relied upon, sometimes as the only evidence of the abuse. Although this is understandable and important, it is critical to understand the process of disclosure,

Common Types of Victim Responses

factors that influence disclosure, and how to present identified "issues" with the victim's disclosures that may be perceived as problematic during the investigation or prosecution process.

General Issues to Remember About Memory

Let's start with some very basic concepts to keep in mind about memory, concepts I find are forgotten by the players in the criminal justice system. We are going to start with a little exercise. Take a moment to think about a week ago Friday. What were you wearing? What did you drink? What did you eat? Who are you with? How long did dinner last? Did you text anyone to tell them about your dinner or where you work? How long were you out? Have you washed your clothes since that time? What time did you go to bed?

This is a difficult exercise. Now try it imagining that you had been raped or beaten that night. And you waited a week to talk about it. And you don't want to talk about it, feel it, or remember it. What do you have access to? In general, people do not go through life encoding irrelevant details in their lives. We take in information all the time, committing only some things to memory. Memory is tremendously complex. It is a reconstruction of our experiences, not a simple reproduction that be replayed by pushing a play, rewind, or pause button. However, investigation often requires a victim to produce minutiae that may have been irrelevant to the experience of that event or that day or the decision to talk about the event. Details of disruptive events, past events, or unimportant aspect of the events may not be accessible to the victim. Although each detail may provide some corroboration or possibility for evidence, it is important to maintain our common sense about memory, as well as to remember that the victim might not want to remember these details or may be desperately avoiding them.

Another important general rule to remember is that repeated interviews will continually increase the likelihood that details can be obtained or contradicted in the interviews. Overall, these details could be irrelevant to the event, especially if those details were difficult for the victim to access in the first place. How long something lasted, what day or time it occurred, how many times it happened, or questions like these might be particularly ripe for contradiction or inconsistencies. In some cases, this could prove that a victim is lying. However, it is more likely that the victim is striving to produce answers that he or she is unsure about. Most people seeking to deceive will have simple, straightforward, and consistent facts lined up for the questions being asked (Rudacille, 1994).

What you are more likely to experience in facing repeated documented disclosures are new details, left-out details, or contradictory details that are not relevant to the allegation of assault itself. In many sexual assault cases I have been involved in, new details emerge when I interview the victim. When the victims are asked why, they commonly answer, "no one ever asked me that." What is important to you as an investigator prosecutor may not be important to the victim or may not be something the victim even understands to be an issue. For example, one young victim never reported that the perpetrator had put his finger in her vagina prior to penetrating her with his penis until the day before trial. That significant "inconsistency" caused some angst in the prosecution team. When asked to explain this omission, the victim simply stated, "I thought this was a rape case. I thought rape was with a penis. I didn't think a finger was part of it."

Inconsistencies in the repetition of the story are an inherent part of the retelling. How victims retell the memory of their assault will be somewhat different each time, as all of our stories that we retell are. Each time I do a training on victim disclosure, using the same slides to make the same points, I talk about the issue a little differently each time, while conveying all the major bullet points on my slides. When a victim is asked to describe an assault, how the story is retold depends on a myriad of things: the victim's state at the time of the telling, who the interviewer is, what triggered the telling, what the context of the questions are, what the purpose of telling is, and more. A victim in a therapy session will disclose differently than a victim being interviewed by a detective or one on the stand in front of the perpetrator. Understanding and planning for this will assist investigators and prosecutors in determining causes for inconsistencies, preparing the victim to explain them, and focusing on the primary issue—the assault.

Finally, many victims have experienced ongoing abuse by a perpetrator. This contributes to a lack of detail for each assault in a discreet way. Victims of ongoing abuse can generally describe a process of the abuse, what it is usually like, and what typically happens. Again, this is common sense. When people are asked to describe a typical course of behavior, they have access to the most recent events and unusual events. For instance, if we use the example of driving to work, people can describe a typical route and a general time frame. Normally, someone would not be able to describe to the minute how long the route took, what traffic was like each day for the past two weeks, or if they hit red lights all the way. Someone might be able to describe experiences that are idiosyncratic, however, like the day they had a car accident or a day that the traffic was unusually awful. In applying this to ongoing sexual abuse or domestic assault, a victim might talk about how she usually got beat when he drank, but she remembered one time in particular that happened near Christmas when he was completely sober. It is important to help victims identify discretionary memories or details that are marked by special events, new behaviors, or unusual circumstances to make the assaults or abuse come to life for the listener. "Mostly it was when mom was at work," she explained. "He would make me go into the bathroom and sit on the toilet. He would put his pee-pee in my mouth and touch me. One day though, mom was home and he did it in the basement." The child went on, "I was so scared she would hear it and be so mad at me!"

Delayed Disclosure

Study after study, victim after victim, and reports from the #Metoo movement confirm that delay of disclosure or not telling all is the most common response to sexual assault or domestic violence by victims. It is estimated that up to 70% of children do not disclose their sexual abuse until reaching adulthood, if they tell it all (Reitsema & Grietens, 2016), and a large portion of adult victims delay or fail to disclose their assaults (Kearns, Edwards, Calhoun, & Gidycz, 2010). It commonly accepted that sexual assault and domestic violence are highly underreported crimes.

The barriers to disclosure have been explored in the previous chapters of this book. Shame, self-blame, ambivalence about or fear of the consequences of telling, and other internal factors prohibit or delay disclosures in victims. Culture can be a strong influence. For example, Latinx show low rates of disclosure of sexual and intimate partner violence. Ahrens and colleagues found that beliefs about marriage, familialism, and taboos about talking about sex, along with prohibitions about sharing family secrets and fear of making the violence worse, all contributed to the victims' unwillingness to disclose (Ahrens, Rios-Mandel, Isas, & del Carmen Lopez, 2010). Male victims disclose less than female victims because of their socialization, fear of being labeled, isolation, and fear of becoming an abuser or being seen as an abuser (Alaggia, 2005; Sorsoli, Kia-Keating, & Grossman, 2008).

Children face significant impediments to disclosure. Most significant is their relationship to the perpetrator. Most children are sexually assaulted by someone with whom they are in a relationship. The closer the relationship, the less likely the child is to disclose, a finding replicated in many studies (Lyon & Ahern, 2011; Reitsema & Grietens, 2016). This is significant given that one of the major goals for the offender is to foster the child's attachment. Offenders obviously understand that attachment, loyalty, and a wish to protect the offender are powerful tools in preventing disclosures of children. Children fear the possible consequences to the family or the offender (Reitsema & Grietens, 2016). "That relationship that the victim and/or the perpetrator might see as a caring relationship even though it was, in the end, a sexual assault, a bad relationship at the end. During the process it was seen as caring," an offender of boys explained to me. Children may face the loss of a very important and giving relationship in their life. The perpetrator might bring presents, money, and food for the family, or may be the sole provider. The abuser might be the child's source of attention and affection. "He thought as though someone was caring for him, that someone had feelings for him, even though those feelings were misguided or going in the wrong direction," an offender explained. The abuser may be an authority to the child, a caretaker for the child, or an important part of the family.

The particular vulnerabilities of the child and his or her family can also contribute to a failure to disclose. Offenders will often choose families with issues or create issues in their own families that promote vulnerability to abuse, both sexual and physical. Social isolation, less-cohesive families, controlling parental styles, inconsistent parenting, or dependency on the abuser are all factors that inhibit disclosure in children being abused (Reitsema & Grietens, 2016). Domestic violence is common in families with sexual abuse; up to 50% of incest perpetrators also batter the children's mother (Bancroft, Silverman, & Ritchie, 2012). Because children typically disclose to a caretaker, having a mother who is in danger, depressed, or otherwise disempowered by domestic violence decreases a child's support resources substantially. And a child's fear of the perpetrator's danger to others can prevent him or her from telling someone outside of the family.

It is important to find ways to help victims disclose abuse. Not only is disclosure a route to stopping the abuse, delayed disclosure has some highly detrimental effects on the victim. Prolonged abuse is certainly one. Delayed disclosure is associated with greater distress, a higher rate of PTSD, self-harm, and other symptoms (Kearns et al., 2010; Ullman, 2007).

Types of Disclosure and the Process of Telling

"It was only disclosed in the end because he talked about it and that conversation was overheard, overheard by someone else," the offender said, explaining how he got caught. Another victim marched into the police station with her T-shirt in a plastic bag. She had saved the offender's semen. "There! Now will you believe me?" the 17-year-old victim asked the officer. This was the third time she had reported being sexually assaulted by her stepfather. "Something weird happened last night, I'm kinda mad about it," another victim texted a friend about her rape by an acquaintance the night before. "Well, I heard him over the phone, screaming and having a fit that he didn't want to go with me. His mother yelled at him to knock it off and be nice. She made him come with me," the offender said, revealing that his last assault of the child was that same day.

All of the above are types of disclosures—purposeful, accidental, piecemeal, or behavioral. Victims disclose or attempt to disclose in many ways, not always in the intentional complete narrative, with the goal of prosecution, that would make investigation much simpler. Alaggia (2004) described four different ways to tell: purposeful, behavioral, intentionally withheld, and triggered. Sometimes victims tell for the purpose of stopping the abuse and exposing the offender (purposeful). Some victims attempt to tell through behavioral issues, like isolation, self-harm, outbursts, or refusal to be with the offender (behavioral). Other victims intentionally withhold disclosure. For some, the disclosure is triggered by an incident, memories, or other events that impel or compel the victim to tell.

Disclosure is a process that occurs over time (London, Bruck, Ceci, & Shuman, 2005; Reitsema & Grietens, 2016). Younger victims disclose more slowly than older victims and are more likely to disclose accidentally (London et al., 2005). Although most research has been conducted on children's disclosure of abuse, this conclusion is supported by adult victims of both domestic violence and sexual assault, in victims' narratives, the literature, and my clinical experience. Disclosure might simply become more comprehensive over time because talking about it becomes easier for the victim. The disclosure process is influenced by a variety of factors, but especially by the listener and trauma.

Interactional Component of Disclosure

"Disclosure is a relational process which is renegotiated by each interaction and evolves over an extended period of time" wrote Reitsema and Grietens (2016) in their review of the literature on disclosure. The process of disclosure for both child and adult victims is greatly impacted by the response and engagement of the listener (London et al., 2005; Reitsema & Grietens, 2016; Sorsoli et al., 2008). Victims will test the listener to whom they want to disclose to assess whether the listener can handle the information, will believe the victims, or will offer support to the victims. Flåm and Haugstvedt (2012) coined the term "test balloons" in relation to how children attempted disclose abuse to their caregiver. They found that, in hindsight, caregivers could identify the child's attempt to communicate abuse. The children rebuffed the abuser, made vague comments, or otherwise tested the listener.

The term "test balloons" is interesting to me in light of the frequency of victims texting to test their listener, their words literally appearing as balloons on the phone screen. Victims will text their friends about something "bad," "upsetting," "weird," or "awkward" that had happened to them, reaching out tentatively to see if the listener is interested, believing, supportive, and would help them figure out how to label their experience. When a direct connection is offered to victims, an open opportunity to discuss abuse by an interested party, victims are more likely to disclose abuse. Caregiver or listener response to initial attempts at disclosure can open or close the door for further disclosure (Reitsmena & Grietens, 2016). If the mother begins to cry, looks angry, or gets very distressed, a child may stop disclosing. If the victim perceives contempt, skepticism, or blame, she may stop telling. In observing one interview of a child, I heard the examiner say, "I'm going to ask your cousin about this—it better be the same thing she says!" The child stopped disclosing.

In a formal interview, the interviewer can have a significant impact on what the victim tells and how they tell it. The interviewer may not even be aware of his impact. For example, I interviewed one victim who stopped talking to the interviewer during the investigation. When I explored this with her, she said, "he was wearing the same cologne as my perpetrator." Initially, the victim was labeled as uncooperative. Asking closed-ended questions or questions only about "the facts, ma'am" can inhibit a victim's full disclosure. The victim may become socialized through the criminal justice process to disregard important details, focusing on only factual elements of the crime and not the experiential. They leave out important information because they're assuming what investigators need to know.

The interviewer can disrupt the process by sticking to a script, demonstrating a rigid inheritance to a protocol, or failing to ask significant questions. A forensic interviewer of a child victim stopped the victim, who was listing all the states in which her father had assaulted her, saying, "wait, wait. Just answer the questions I asked you. I asked you to spell your name." Victims who are able to at least start with their own narrative can provide a significant amount of information that can be followed up on by an interviewer who is willing to listen. Blaming questions, questions focused on the victim's choices and behaviors, or questions revealing disbelief can all shut down a victim and make him or her unwilling to participate.

Victims may reveal more information over time. This is sometimes referred to as "piecemeal disclosure," when the victim's narrative about the abuse or assault becomes more detailed and comprehensive. Obviously, this is often interpreted as inconsistent disclosure. The addition of details or clarification of issues may be a direct result of the skill or interest of the interviewer. Many, many times I have heard, "no one ever asked me that." However, this process also can be impacted by victims' feeling of shame, self-blame, or fear of not being believed. The victim may protect the offender, not wanting to reveal things that may be embarrassing or may paint the offender in the worst light. The victim may disclose more after being educated more. For example, a child in therapy may begin to understand the offender's grooming process and then be able to convey that to investigators. The victims may fail to report certain things that they think make them look bad, like they deserve to be assaulted. After some time and support, the victim may be able to report these things with a decreased sense of blame. Again, given the interactional nature of disclosure, the listener can do things to decrease the victim's reluctance to disclose by being an active, supportive, and nonjudgmental listener.

When a victim receives a negative response from the listener, it is not only likely to shut down the disclosure but also can leave the victim with more scars than the abuse itself! For children, being disbelieved by a trusted caretaker can be worse than the actual assault or abuse (Reitsema & Grietens, 2016; Ullman, 2007). Victims who fear a negative reaction or disbelief from authorities will not even make a police report (Ahrens, 2006).

Trauma and Disclosure

The victims often are disclosing a chaotic, distressing, and traumatic event to the interviewer. During the disclosure process, the victim might be experiencing symptoms of trauma, including intrusive memories, flashbacks, or physical feelings of the assault. They may have significant anxiety, fear, or terror at reliving the event. The victim might be experiencing dissociative symptoms during the disclosure. Dissociation and other symptoms related to PTSD can be triggered by the retelling of the assault (Alaggia, 2005; Allen, 2005). This is a common expectation in clinical work with victims. It is important for investigators and prosecutors at least to be aware of the potential for the experience of trauma and its symptoms to be part of the disclosure process. Memories of the traumatic event are the primary source of emotional distress for victims. The victim may not be able to share certain details or parts of the assault because it is too emotionally distressing or causes actual physical illness. In a clinical setting and during trial, I have seen victims throw up, faint, or have pseudoseizures that are due to the stress of reliving the assault or abuse.

Triggers for Disclosure

Interviewers have often asked, as have researchers, "why didn't you tell?" A more important question is "what made you tell?" Disclosures are triggered for victims who might have never planned to tell for a variety of reasons. Although the barriers to disclosure have been well studied, the facilitators for disclosure have been less so.

Opportunity and Social Support

In two studies, being afforded opportunities to tell helped the victims disclose (Malloy, Brubacher, & Lamb, 2013; Sorsoli et al., 2008). These opportunities were provided by being alone with a trusted adult, watching a television show on sexual abuse, or being talked to or directly educated about abuse. These findings highlight the general avoidance of the topic of abuse and related education for children. When no one talks about it, it is hard to bring up and tell. Children are better able to disclose when offered some common connection to the abuse by a caretaker who does not try to offer excuses or rationalizations for the abuse. A listener who expresses disbelief or has a negative emotional response to the child can also be problematic (Malloy et al., 2013; Reitsema & Grietens, 2016).

New or increased social supports facilitate disclosure and help-seeking in both adult and child victims of violence, especially if that person is perceived as being empowered to help (Davies, Block, & Campbell, 2007; McCart, Smith, & Sawyer, 2010; Reitsema & Grietens, 2016). Not only does good informal social support help facilitate disclosures, it increases the chances of the victim participating in prosecution (Anders & Christopher, 2011).

Increased Needs of the Victim

Another reason for disclosure includes injury or medical needs, like sexually transmitted diseases or pregnancy or increased or unremitting psychological symptoms (McCart et al., 2010). "I thought I could, you know, just get over it, forget about it. But eight months later, I was still sleeping on the couch," the victim explained. "I still couldn't have sex with my husband. He was always asking what was wrong." Male victims in particular will seek help for injuries sustained during a sexual assault (Tewksbury, 2007).

Increased Knowledge of the Victim

The victim's increased knowledge can trigger disclosure. Education about sexual abuse for children (Rietsema & Grietens, 2016), better information about resources or options (McCart et al., 2010; NCAVP, 2010; NDVH, 2015), or identification of the assault as a crime (Donne et al., 2018) all facilitate disclosure. Labeling the experience as a crime, rape, assault, or abuse facilitates help-seeking and disclosure in both men and women (Donne et al., 2018; Littleton, Axsom, Breitkopf, & Berenson, 2006), since those who do not label their experiences accurately do not seek help for these experiences. "Why would I report it? I didn't know it was rape—it was just bad," explained a young rape victim. "I was ashamed I couldn't get over it. I didn't know what it was until I went to counseling." A victim of severe emotional abuse, then physical abuse, said, "I didn't see it coming. Really. He said terrible things to me, but I didn't know it was abuse." The language that investigators and prosecutors use with the victims can facilitate this increased knowledge. Asking a victim about the "sex they had" is vastly different than asking about the sexual assault. Referring to an offender's physical assault (thus crime) to a victim will reframe something that she might be thinking of as an "argument" or her batterer losing his temper.

Another important piece of information is knowledge of or protection of other victims. One adolescent told me, "I knew I finally had to tell. I saw the way he started looking at my sister. I thought 'oh, no, not her too.'" Many times in my work with military sexual assault cases, more victims would come forward once they were inspired by the identification of another victim. "Well," she said, "if she could do it, I can do it. I mean, how many more are out there?" It seems that the knowledge of other victims frees the victim from the personalization of the abuse. It is no longer something that he or she provoked from the perpetrator in a vacuum. The victim can better identify the behavior as the offender's problem, as opposed to something that happened between the two of them. "When I started hearing about what he did to some other people in the barracks, I could finally say it wasn't me," a victim said. Another young man said, "I mean, I thought it was something I asked for, that I was special to him. When I found out about the others, I realized he was just a sick fuck, some pervert preying on us." When children are exposed to the risks of domestic violence, victims make the decision to disclose for the protection of the children (Buchanan, Power, & Verity, 2013), though this might make the victim vulnerable to accusations of false allegations (Bancroft et al., 2012).

Removal From the Perpetrator or Changes in the Abuser's Behavior

Disclosure may be triggered when the victim is removed from the perpetrator's influence. Children might tell after a separation or divorce, both because they feel safer and because they may be afraid to be alone with the perpetrator in a custody situation. Victims of intimate abuse disclose when they are leaving, perhaps out of fear of the reprisal for leaving or as an explanation for it. Victims in the military often disclose when they leave the military, change duty stations, or leave a unit. Victims of domestic violence decide to disclose because of an escalation of the abuse in severity or frequency or because of the appearance of other abusive behaviors of the offender (Davies et al., 2007). "I was never going to tell," a victim of violence said. "Until he strangled me. I thought, 'This is it. Who is going to raise my children?' Then I knew I needed help." Victims of child sexual abuse might disclose if the offender becomes more abusive or punitive. "A month, a month and a half later, I punished her for something and she told her mother what I've done," an offender said, reiterating a common experience among offenders.

Trauma and Memory

The neurobiology of assault or of a traumatic event is highly complex. I will not address it here. However, I will describe some basic concepts of the impact of trauma on memory and therefore affecting the disclosure process. First, trauma is not a diagnosis. It is generally defined as a highly distressing, possibly life-threatening event, or the lasting impact of that event. Sexual and physical assault are events that can produce trauma and produce a traumatic impact on memory.

Traumatic memory is not like normal memory. During an assault, the brain is flooded with chemicals from many glands, some of which have the responsibility for survival, flight, or fight responses (Campbell, 2012). The process of encoding memory gets disorganized and overwhelmed; some of the released chemicals make it more difficult for the structures responsible for organizing and encoding memory to work (Campbell, 2012). At a very basic physiological level, assault can compromise memory. It disorganizes the brain so that decision-making is difficult as well. As the victim is surviving the assault, the victim's brain is struggling with an onslaught of chemicals in an effort to understand and encode an event that is horrible. Campbell (2012) describes the brain's efforts as the same as trying to write down a lecture on small pieces of paper, then scattering those little pages all over, and trying to reorganize them correctly. The victim struggles with organizing fragments that can be confusing or overwhelming (Allen, 2005). Traumatic events are associated with periods of forgetting or failure to recall the event at all, called traumatic amnesia, in a significant percentage of victims (American Psychiatric Association, 2013).

This does not imply that the memory overall is not accurate. Experiential memory can be highly accurate, even in very young children (Allen, 2005; Campbell, 2012; Hewitt, 1999). Using the small-pieces example just presented, the words the victim has written on those little pieces is accurate—it is just that those pieces might not all be in the right order. A victim will try to recall as best she can, perhaps being reminded of what pieces go together. This "piecemeal" or fragmented process of telling does not represent lying or deception, but the actual product of our biology in relation to trauma. And the victim is *always* sure that the traumatic event happened, but perhaps does not have access to the peripheral details.

As mentioned earlier, a victim might be engaged in active efforts not to remember as well. The psychological defenses of dissociation and depersonalization can come into play. These defenses disrupt the normal integration of cognitive function, including memory, perception, consciousness, and behavior, often following a traumatic event (American Psychiatric Association, 2013). Dissociation is the loss of the continuity of conscious experience or the inability to access information or the psychological or behavioral controls that are normally accessible. Victims will describe this as "blanking out" or "checking out." Depersonalization is the feeling of detachment from oneself, like watching a third party, while derealization is the feeling that things are unreal or like a dream. Although these defenses are typically involuntary, a victim might purposefully fantasize, daydream, or attempt to escape the reality of the trauma. "I would stare into my closet and organize all my stuffed animals in my mind," one girl told me. "Or I would daydream about what I would be when I grew up." Another adult victim said, "I would hear his shoes coming down the hallway and the next thing I knew it would be the next day. I know he abused me, sometimes I could smell it. But I can't tell you what happened."

When interviewing a victim, it is imperative to understand some of these concepts, even at a basic level. Law enforcement officers are trained to interrogate, look for deception, and ask questions in a manner to "trip up" the accused. The general rules of deception detection cannot apply to victims of trauma. Even basic premises of "lie detection" or deception are impacted by trauma. "Inconsistencies," failures in memory, reticence, and body language that suggests deception, like hiding or blocking behaviors, will be demonstrated by victims experiencing trauma.

Recantation

After a conviction, I overheard a very bold offender ask his attorney, "if she takes it back again, can I walk?" This offender was convicted of assaulting his stepdaughter, who had disclosed but recanted, allowing him more years to abuse her. Luckily, she told again. Recantation is a victim behavior dreaded by investigators and prosecutors. Although it can be used as a term to describe when a victim "takes back" a lie, it is used in research as a term to describe when a victim retracts or denies prior allegations of substantiated abuse. It is something that happens with child victims and with a significant portion of IPV victims. Some posit that up to 80% of IPV victims will recant (Meier, 2006). Recantation contributes to the confusion, frustration, and helplessness of prosecutors, investigators, and helpers.

Recantation in children is associated with specific things. Studies have shown that recantation can occur between 20%–30% of the time in situations that have increased risk of recantation (Lyon & Ahern, 2011). Malloy and colleagues found that risk issues included removal from the home post-disclosure, removal from siblings post-disclosure, nonoffending caregiver disbelief, exposure to family pressure, and visitation or contact with the abuser (Malloy, Mugno, Rivard, Lyon, & Quas, 2016). These similar risk factors are supported by earlier research. In addition, a close relationship to the perpetrator can be a factor (London et al., 2005; Lyon & Ahern, 2011). Since most children disclose to a parent, usually their mother, a mother's disbelief is incredibly powerful. Understanding these factors has significant implications for foster care, visitation, and situations in which accused perpetrators are not confined before conviction.

Recantation of victims in cases of domestic violence is a serious issue as well. Not only does it confound prosecution, but it endangers the victim. Some concrete factors that can trigger recantation in these victims include: financial dependence on the abuser, substance abuse of the victim, a victim's failure to label the abuse a crime, the victim's fear that things will get worse by reporting, and the victim's poor experience with the criminal justice system. More intangible is the offender's influence on the victim. This can include threats or coercion, apologies, acceptance of responsibility, or promises to change (Roberts, Wolfer, & Mele, 2008). Bonomi and colleagues studied prison phone calls to better understand the offenders' influence on the victims' recantation (Bonomi, Gangamma, Locke, Katafiasz, & Martin, 2011). They found a multistep process in which the offender elicits sympathy; minimizes the offenses; invokes the attachment, loss, and hope in the relationship; and then asks the victim to recant, citing their better future together and characterizing the prosecutors as the common enemy.

Despite the prevalence of recantation and success of offenders at instigating recantation, law enforcement and prosecutors are fighting back by charging offenders with witness tampering, obstruction, or other related charges when evidence of this is reported or uncovered. Additionally, evidence-based prosecution is gaining momentum. This type of prosecution does not rely on a victim's disclosure, but trains investigators and prosecutors to gather evidence from the very beginning of the case to enable them to go forward without the victim.

Secondary Victimization as a Result of Disclosure

Secondary victimization by disclosing is a real risk for victims of abuse. Secondary victimization is described as the traumatization of victims because of the disbelief, biases, myth acceptance, victim blaming, and maltreatment by law enforcement, help providers, and other players in the prosecutorial process, including attorneys.

Law-enforcement attitudes and the potential to create secondary victimization have been examined in a number of studies. There persists a belief in law enforcement that false allegations of assault occur at a high rate, when the actual rate a false allegations is less than 10% (Lisak, Gardinier, Nicksa, & Cote, 2010; Mennicke, Anderson, Oehme, & Kennedy, 2014). Even if the officers indicate they don't believe rape or domestic violence myths, officers make decisions about victim credibility that could result in a significantly detrimental impact to the victim and reporting of assault. Page (2007) found that officers in her study were less likely to believe prostitutes and men reporting sexual assault, though they believed both could be raped.

The impact of the negative attitudes of officers is likely to have a far greater impact on the victim than attitudes of the general population

(Sleath & Bull, 2017), since the victim relies on the officers for assistance and investigation. This study, too, found that myths and negative attitudes toward victims impacted officers' assessment of victim credibility (Sleath & Bull, 2017). Officer's biases and perpetuation of rape myths appear from the very start of the investigation—in the report writing. A study by Shaw and colleagues, examined police reports on sexual assault, which contained conclusions that the victim was lying and comments on victim behavior, status, or injury that reflected rape myths. From the start, the officers stated that the victims were lying, "didn't act like a victim," or presented a "weak" case. The implications on prosecution of these findings are profound. The good news is that training focused on education and amelioration of these beliefs and biases has been successful (Darwinkel, Powell, & Tidmarsh, 2013).

Victim of intimate partner violence suffer the same, if not more, risk of secondary victimization for disclosing the abuse. Because the victim has chosen to have ongoing contact with the perpetrator, she can be held responsible for her own abuse by helpers and law enforcement. Policastro and Payne (2013) found that studies showed that victims of domestic violence are blamed by some respondents for not leaving the abusers sooner and are considered to have consented to the abuse by not leaving, and in fact to have wanted to be abused. The theme of the victim provoking the abuse also appeared in the research. The idea that victims provoke the abuse is widespread. When Ray Rice assaulted his wife in an elevator, knocking her out, a prosecutor I was discussing it with said, "well, she shouldn't have poked the bear!" When sexual assault occurs in the context of intimate partner violence, the victim can face even more blaming and disbelief.

It is important to remember the secondary victimization during a trial as well. The process of prosecution is rife with the elements that can produce secondary victimization; for instance, cross-examination or closing arguments. Throughout the process of investigation and prosecution, the victim needs to be prepared for and supported against this in order to ensure the victim's cooperation and prevent further harm in the pursuit of justice. Use of victim advocates, victim witness liaisons, and the victims' social support system can be useful. More importantly, it is important to provide education and training to prevent secondary victimization from occurring early in the investigation process through the behavior of help providers and law enforcement officers.

Summary

Disclosure is a process, one that is influenced by many factors. The role of the listener, the impact of trauma, and the consequences of disclosure are critical either in facilitating it or in shutting it down. Barriers to disclosure are numerous, the hurdles seeming sometimes insurmountable for victims.

Response of helpers and law enforcement can not only hinder disclosure but cause secondary trauma for the victim. Remember these important points:

- Disclosure does not happen all at once; the process is mitigated by
  - The victim's feelings and beliefs;
  - Cultural issues and values;
  - Developmental stages;
  - Trauma;
  - The interviewer or listener; and
  - The consequences of telling.
- We have faulty expectations of victim memory generally, notwithstanding the impact of trauma.
- Trauma has a basic physiological impact on the encoding, organization, and retrieval of memory.
- The victim might experience or engage in specific defenses against forming memories of an assault.
- There are many things that can enhance the likelihood of disclosure, including opportunity for, education of, and support for the victim.
- Recantation does not mean the end of a case. Evidence-based prosecution and other means are available to pursue justice.
- Victims are not offenders. Training in interrogation techniques is not only misleading when working with victims, it can be damaging.

Finally, education and training about disclosure of intimate violence is imperative for interviewers and prosecutors and effective at minimizing errors regarding victim disclosure.

References

Ahrens, C. E. (2006). Being silenced: The impact of negative social reactions on the disclosure of rape. *American Journal of Community Psychology, 38,* 263–274. doi:10.1007/s10464-006-9069-9

Ahrens, C. E., Rios-Mandel, L. C., Isas, L., & del Carmen Lopez, M. (2010). Talking about interpersonal violence: Cultural influences on Latinas' identification and disclosure of sexual assault and intimate partner violence. *Psychological Trauma: Theory, Research, Practice, and Policy, 2*(4), 284–295. doi:10.1037/a0018605

Alaggia, R. (2004). Many ways of telling: Expanding conceptualizations of child sexual abuse disclosure. *Child Abuse and Neglect, 28,* 1213–1227.

Alaggia, R. (2005). Disclosing the trauma of child sexual abuse: A gender analysis. *Journal of Loss and Trauma, 10,* 453–470.

Allen, J. (2005). *Coping with trauma: Hope through understanding.* Washington, DC: American Psychiatric Association.

American Psychiatric Association. (2013). *Diagnostic and statistical manual of mental disorders* (5th ed.). Arlington, VA: American Psychiatric Association.

Anders, M., & Christopher, F. (2011). A socioecological model of rape survivor's decisions to aid in case prosecution. *Psychology of Women Quarterly, 35*, 92–106. doi:10.1177/0361684310394802

Bancroft, L., Silverman, J., & Ritchie, D. (2012). *The batterer as parent: Addressing the impact of domestic violence on family dynamics*. Los Angeles, CA: Sage.

Bonomi, A. E., Gangamma, R., Locke, C. R., Katafiasz, H., & Martin, D. (2011). "Meet me at the hill where we used to park": Interpersonal processes associated with victim recantation. *Social Science & Medicine, 73*, 1054–1061.

Buchanan, F., Power, C., & Verity, F. (2013). Domestic violence and the place of fear in mother/baby relationships: "What was I afraid of ? Of making it worse". *Journal of Interpersonal Violence, 28*, 1817–1838. doi:10.1177/0886260 512469108

Campbell, R. (2012, December 3). The neurobiology of sexual assault. *An NIJ Research for the Real World Seminar*. National Institute of Justice: US Department of Justice. Retrieved from www.nij.gov/multimedia/presenter/presenter-campbell/Pages/welcome.aspx

Darwinkel, E., Powell, M., & Tidmarsh, P. (2013). Improving police officers' perceptions of sexual offending through intensive training. *Criminal Justice and Behavior, 40*, 895–908. doi:10.1177/0093854813475348

Davies, K., Block, C., & Campbell, J. (2007). Seeking help from police: Battered women's decisions and experiences. *Criminal Justice Studies, 20*, 15–41. doi:10/1080/14786010701241317

Donne, M., DeLuca, J., Pleskach, P., Bromson, C., Mosley, M., Perez, E., . . . Frye, V. (2018). Barriers to and facilitators of help-seeking behavior among men who experience sexual violence. *American Journal of Men's Health, 12*(2), 189–201. doi:10.1177/155798831774066

Flåm, A. M., & Haugstvedt, E. (2012). Test balloons? Small signs of big events: A qualitative study on circumstances facilitating adults' awareness of children's first signs of sexual abuse. *Child Abuse & Neglect, 37*, 633–642.

Hewitt, S. (1999). *Assessing allegations of sexual abuse in preschool children: Understanding small voices*. Thousand Oaks, CA: Sage.

Kearns, M., Edwards, K., Calhoun, K., & Gidycz, C. (2010). Disclosure of sexual victimization: The effects of pennebaker's emotional disclosure paradigm on physical and psychological distress. *Journal of Trauma & Dissociation, 11*(2), 193–209.

Lisak, D., Gardinier, L., Nicksa, S., & Cote, A. (2010). False allegations of sexual assault: An analysis of ten years of reported cases. *Violence Against Women, 16*(12), 1318–1343. doi:10.1177/1077801210387747

Littleton, H., Axsom, D., Breitkopf, C., & Berenson, A. (2006). Rape acknowledgement and postassault experiences: How acknowledgment status relates to disclosure, coping, worldview, and reactions received from others. *Violence and Victims, 21*(6), 761–778.

London, K., Bruck, M., Ceci, S., & Shuman, D. (2005). Disclosure of child sexual abuse: What does the research tell us about the ways that children tell? *Psychology, Public Policy, & Law, 11*(1), 194–226. doi:10.1037/1076-8971.11.1.194

Lyon, T. D., & Ahern, E. C. (2011). Disclosure of child sexual abuse. In J. Myers (Ed.), *The APSAC handbook on child maltreatment* (3rd ed., pp. 233–252). Newbury Park, CA: Sage.

Malloy, L. C., Brubacher, S. P., & Lamb, M. E. (2013). "Because she's one who listens": Children discuss disclosure recipients in forensic interviews. *Child Maltreatment, 18*, 245–251. doi:10.1177/1077559513497250

Malloy, L. C., Lyon, T., & Quas, J. (2007). Filial dependency and recantations of child sexual abuse allegations. *Journal of the American Academy of Child & Adolescent Psychiatry, 46*(2), 162–170. doi:10.1097/01.chi.0000246067.77953.f7

Malloy, L. C., Mugno, A., Rivard, J., Lyon, T., & Quas, J. (2016). Familial influences on recantation in substantiated child sexual abuse cases. *Child Maltreatment, 21*(3), 256–261. doi:10.1177/1077559516650936

McCart, M., Smith, D., & Sawyer, G. (2010). Help seeking among victims of crime: A review of the empirical literature. *Journal of Traumatic Stress, 23*, 198–206. doi:10.1002/jts.20509

Meier, J. S. (2006). Davis/Hammon, domestic violence, and the supreme court: The case for cautious optimism. *First Impressions, 22*, 22–27.

Mennicke, A., Anderson, D., Oehme, K., & Kennedy, S. (2014). Law enforcement officers' perception of rape and rape victims: A multimethod study. *Violence and Victims, 29*(5), 815–827.

National Domestic Violence Hotline. (2015). *Who will help me? Domestic violence survivors speak out about law enforcement responses.* Washington, DC. Retrieved from www.thehotline.org/resources/law-enforcement-responses

NCAVP. (2010). *Hate violence against the LGBTQ communities in the U.S. in 2009.* Retrieved from https://avp.org/wp-content/uploads/2017/04/2011_NCAVP_HV_Reports.pdf

Page, A. D. (2007). Behind the blue line: Investigating police officers' attitudes toward rape. *Journal of Police and Criminal Psychology, 22*(1), 22–32.

Policastro, C., & Payne, B. (2013). The blameworthy victim: Domestic violence myths and criminalization of victimhood. *Journal of Aggression, Maltreatment, & Trauma, 22*, 329–347. doi:10.1080/10926771.2013.775985

Reitsema, A., & Grietens, H. (2016). Is anybody listening? The literature on the dialogical process of child sexual abuse disclosure reviewed. *Trauma, Violence, & Abuse, 17*(3), 330–340. doi:10.1177/1524838015584368

Roberts, J. C., Wolfer, L., & Mele, M. (2008). Why victims of intimate partner violence withdraw protection orders. *Journal of Family Violence, 23*, 369e375.

Rudacille, W. (1994). *Identifying lies in disguise.* Dubuque, IA: Kendall Hunt.

Sleath, E., & Bull, R. (2017). Police perceptions of rape victims and the impact on case decision making: A systematic review. *Aggression and Violent Behavior, 34*, 102–112. doi:10.1016/j.avb.2017.02.003

Sorsoli, L., Kia-Keating, M., & Grossman, F. (2008). "I keep that hush-hush": Male survivors of sexual abuse and challenges of disclosure. *Journal of Counseling Psychology, 55*(3), 333–345. doi:10.1037/0022–0167.55.3.333

Tewksbury, R. (2007). Effects of sexual assaults on men: Physical, mental, and sexual consequences. *International Journal of Men's Health, 6*(1), 22–35. doi:10.3149/jmh.0601.22

Ullman, S. (2007). Relationship to perpetrator, disclosure, social reactions, and PTSD symptoms in child sexual abuse survivors, *Journal of Child Sexual Abuse, 16*(1), 19–36. doi:10.1300/J070v16n01_02

Chapter 7

"But I Love Him"
Continued Contact With the Offender

This counselor questions why student waited over one month to disclose. Also, mom reports that student's relationship with step-dad has been amicable.
—Report by guidance counselor after disclosure of abuse by student

So I am suffering and my defense mechanism wants me to pull away but I can't bc I love you.
—Text from victim of rape and assault by a boyfriend

The goal was obvious: to suggest that Constand had lied when she told police their contact after the night in question was limited and to plant the idea that a woman who had been sexually assaulted would not have keep up contact with her abuser.
—NBC News, June 6, 2017

Return to the marriage. Post-assault text messages. Consensual sex with the perpetrator after a reported rape. Going to breakfast together after the night of abuse. Going to work the next day after the supervisor sexually assaults the victim in the supply closet. All of these are examples of continued contact with the offender, a victim behavior that frustrates prosecutors and baffles jurors. Why does she go back? Why doesn't she leave? How could he love him? Victims tend to display the most "counterintuitive" behaviors in situations when there is relationship with the offender.

Relationships as the Weapon of the Offender

Most people who are victimized are victimized by someone they know. This is well established and previously discussed. Let's consider why this is from the offender's point of view. It is "counterintuitive" that a criminal would place him- or herself in a position to be identified criminally and give the victim evidence—DNA, text messages, photos, love letters, even confessions. Why would he do this? Isn't easier to meet the needs of abuse and rage, whether sexual or physical, with a stranger? Absolutely not. Relationships are generally necessary for the successful offender, especially one who wants full access to a victim. In fact, the closer the offender is to the victim, the more crimes that offender can commit against that victim. Imagine a father abusing the child over years. In my practice, I have the offenders estimate the number of sex crimes they have committed against their victim; sometimes the estimates are in the thousands. This differs from the offender with a more distant relationship to the victim, one in which he can "only" commit one or a few crimes against his chosen victim. A relationship is an effective vehicle for intimate crimes because it provides access to the victim, provides excuses and explanations for the offense, is used against the victims, and establishes status issues.

Access to the Victim

It is difficult to gain access to victims without some sort of expectation of contact and cooperation, which is easily established in the context of a relationship, however brief. The relationship provides the offender access to the victim. A stranger does not belong in your bed no matter what, but a date in your bedroom is not so glaringly problematic. A man does not bathe a stranger's child but is a good father when bathing his own. Some type of prior contact or acquaintanceship gives the offender an opportunity to exploit the victim's trust and affiliation. "When we saw each other again, in a different city where I barely knew anyone, I readily accepted his invitation to a party at his friend's house. It was there, after lots of laughter and many more drinks, that he leaned in for a kiss—and my world was turned upside down," a victim explained (Antonova, 2017). Offenders of children understand that forming attachment and a relationship with their victims is critical to their success (Katz & Barnetz, 2016).

There are certain contexts that accelerate the perception of a relationship. Social media, the socialization to "family" and "team" that exists in the military or in athletics, or going through an unusual event together all hasten a victim's perception that a relationship exists, even if the offender is a stranger. I have evaluated many, many offenders who understood this very well, "friending" their victims on Facebook, luring them somewhere, and raping them. Even the term "friending" captures the assumption of a benevolent connection. The context of the military that refers to "brothers and sisters in arms," accelerating bonding and trust among young soldiers. Many times I have heard from victims, "I am supposed to trust a fellow soldier with my life. We are a family. I never thought I would be raped by one." The term fraternity "brothers" evokes the belief that intimacy, trust, and a relationship exists, when in fact the people are strangers to one another until significant time has passed.

In a situation of intimate partner violence, the more established the relationship is and the more involved the offender's and victim's lives are, the greater access the offender has to the victim. The offender likely lives in the victim's home—the place that is supposed to be safe. These offenders often will wait to reveal their violence until the relationship and interdependence is solidly established by living together, marriage, or children. "He was fantastic until our honeymoon," a victim of intimate partner violence said. "The very first night was the first time he beat me. When I begged him to tell me why, he said, 'I have you now.'"

Provides Excuses and Explanations for the Abuse

Without a relationship, an offender has a difficult time explaining away or giving excuses for the offense behavior. Offenders continuously rely on the interactions with the victim to defend themselves or to camouflage their behaviors and intentions. "I told her to put on her pajamas and get ready for bed and I had my shorts off because I got wet from the bath, and she just grabbed it! I swear to God, I just lost it for a minute," one offender insisted to his wife when she caught him with his penis in his four-year-old's mouth. An offender of adolescent girls explained, "yeah, I would walk into the bath house where I knew they were changing, say sorry, when I knew damn well they were in there." He was able to successfully peep many times. Whether the offender is contending that the victim flirted, consented, provoked, or misunderstood the abuse, the offender must rely on the relationship for these victim blaming positions. It would be difficult for an offender to blame the victim in a stranger-rape scenario, saying, "Well, her car broke down! What was I supposed to do? Not rape her?"

A relationship with the victim is used to by the offender to cite motives for the victim to lie about the abuse or assault. Without interactions with the victim, it would be difficult for the offender to claim that the victim was retaliating for betrayal, seeking vengeance for something, had "buyer's remorse," or was "crying rape" to cover up infidelity. It would be challenging to explain the emotional investment required for retaliation or vengeance from a stranger. It would be much harder, too, to confuse a stranger by altering the truth of the assault. The relationship not only allows the offender to influence the victim's truth, but the access with which to do it. "You were acting like a crazy person," one offender wrote his victim. "You started to kick and wiggle. I had to use a more uncomfortable method to restrain you." He added, "I was not choking you. I had you in a hold that caused you to choke yourself." It would be hard to imagine a stranger leaving a letter explaining his rape and assault by blaming the victim.

Through having a relationship with the victim, the offender has connections around the victim as well. These are necessary for grooming the environment. The offender can surround himself with advocates and witnesses who can "prove" the victim is lying, crazy, or vindictive. This can include children, especially in cases of domestic violence, when the offender can turn the children against the victim. "I should have given your mother an opportunity to explain herself, but I was so angry and hurt that I let my feelings and temper get out of control in that moment," an offender wrote to his children who witnessed him batter their mother. He goes on to talk about how their mother was wrong and he was hurt but couldn't forgive himself for "getting mad." This subtle manipulation of the two young children clearly portrayed him as the wronged victim who lashed out only because he was so hurt by the mother's actions. The children could easily blame the mother for causing their father's behavior. Offenders use third parties all the time against the victims, to pressure, retaliate, take the offender's side, and provide information to investigators that create disbelief and doubt about the victim. "Barracks whore," "crazy," "bitch," "cold," or "liar" are all things I have heard third parties say about victims in defense of the offender. In fact, often when I or prosecutors question these witnesses where they learned someone was "bipolar" or "lied all the time," they will say (without hesitation), "oh, [the offender] told me all about it!"

Used Against the Victim

"You don't want to send daddy to jail, do you?" "Why would you ruin his career with this report?" "You are going to take him away from his kids!" These and many other things have been said to victims by the offender and others to shift the burden of the crimes and the consequences to the victims of intimate violence. The offender instrumentally utilizes the care, love, guilt, and protection offered by the victim to ensure the victim's silence and compliance. The relationship that the offender garners with the victim becomes the victim's responsibility to maintain and tend to. Bill Cosby often called his victim, Andrea Constand. She returned his calls and this was used against her at trial. In an explanation for her calls, she said she felt like she had to answer and return calls from Cosby so she wouldn't "stir up trouble" (Connor, 2017). "She was invested in me, we had kids, I didn't think she was she was going to leave me," another abuser indicated. Even when victims decide to contact the police at some time in the relationship, they are often blamed for not leaving earlier (Payne & Gainey, 2009, cited in Policastro & Payne, 2013).

Consent is another issue that the offender exploits in a relationship. Forced sex is very common in abusive relationships, with the victims being reluctant to label it rape or assault. Only about 50% of sexually victimized women label their experience of forced sex as an assault, and the rate of assault is much higher when committed by intimate partners

(Logan, Walker, & Cole, 2015). As a relationship goes on, consent becomes implicit. We then begin to think about consent being revoked rather than given (Logan et al., 2015). Imagine if you lent your car to someone, then they just took it all the time. Many people still believe in "wifely duties" or marital rights, even that a "husband can't rape a wife." It is shocking how modern marital rape laws are, because of the idea that consent is implicit. In fact, however, sexual assault in a relationship is a lethality indicator as well as highly traumatic for the victim.

Even though the offenders have risked everything to commit their crimes, the victims are always the ones confronted about ruining things. The offender blackmails the victim in the relationship, whether by threats or by invoking the failure to be a good person. The victim is required to forgive, understand, and have empathy and sympathy; be a good Christian by turning the other cheek; and provide second, third, or fourth chances. The offender places that victim in a position to be angry, hostile, hurt, or vindictive, then uses these feelings against the victim. Society does the same, requiring that the victim be both a "good person" who honors the relationship and someone who has the ability to shut these qualities off when she is supposed to leave the abuser, be angry, and seek justice. The victims are given mixed messages from the offender and the community about the relationship to the offender.

> *I was told I should kiss the ground that he walked on because no one would want me, that I would get raped and killed if I ever left him, that I would lose the kids because no judge would ever give custody to a crippled.*

This is from a woman who was forced at gunpoint to suck her son's penis. She was convicted as a sexual offender and served significant jail time. She was sentenced more heavily for her act than her husband's ongoing terrorization of her and the children, in part because she did not leave him.

Establishes Status Issues

Perhaps at no other time has the power of status been so glaringly highlighted than in the sexual assault allegations against Harvey Weinstein, Bill Cosby, the Catholic Church, Larry Nassar, Jerry Sandusky, and others. In these cases, the victims experienced the established status issues of the offender—the Hollywood mogul who could make or break her, the doctor who could disqualify her, the priest who could condemn him, and on and on. Antonova (2017) wrote about her rapist, "I would be cast out. I would be branded a hysterical bitch, a liar, and a jealous fraud who wanted to ruin a great man of letters. Who would want to work with me after that?" She went on to describe how the rapist helped her by networking with her, describing her as talented to others, and introducing her to people in his network who could help her.

Offenders understand their status. They know about their power over the victim and the community, whether it is positive or established through fear and threats. Parents understand their power over their children. Offenders understand their value in the context of the relationship with the victim and their community. One offender who was an attorney stated,

> *I wore the white hat and a lot of different roles I had the role of being a prosecutor which comes with certain trust, public trust, trust of the coworkers. I was in charge of putting bad guys away, so no one looks at you like you're the bad guy. And I wore the white hat, volunteering with the church youth group. There's a certain level of trust in that community that's inherent in the values and principles that are taught in the church community, like forgiveness and redemption.*

Why Doesn't She Leave? The Meaning of the Relationship to the Victim

When I googled "why doesn't she leave," there were more than a trillion results. This seems like an age-old question that gets relentlessly revisited, and never more than in the criminal justice system. The issue is complex and applicable generally to those victimized by someone they are attached to—issues magnified and exacerbated by love, hope, dependency, and fear. There are many more comprehensive resources on the subject, but here are a few that are important to understand and present during trial.

Practical Matters

Perhaps the easiest issues to explain are the concrete, practical issues. Victims can have continued contact with an offender out of necessity, whether they are married or simply acquaintances. These issues are often understood by juries *if the juries are reminded of them.* The practical, common-sense answers should always be highlighted. An investigator needs to gather the information and the prosecutor needs to directly address these issues. It should never be assumed that people will simply identify and understand these things. Here are some examples:

- Resources—The victim might not have money, gas, car, keys, important documents, driver's license, or a support system. Offenders control resources effectively.
- Children—Leaving children might not be an option and having them binds the victims' freedom. It can include waking children in the

night, alerting the offender about potential custody issues or loss, legal ramifications, taking children from school, loss of family, and more.

- Being a child—Children do not have a choice in who they are made to come into contact with, especially when they have not disclosed.
- Employment—A victim might not have employment or might risk losing employment with what leaving may entail. A victim who is employed with the perpetrator faces a job loss or retaliation at work for reporting. If the victim is in the military, the choice of avoiding the perpetrator may be highly restricted.
- Pets—A victim might fear for the safety of a pet or not want the loss of a pet. Leaving without a pet or with a pet involves another level of decision-making.
- Location—If a victim is in a small town, small subgroup, or the same church as the offender, or otherwise isolated with the offender, this could be an issue. A victim who is in a town with only two grocery stores likely will have contact with the offender.

It is not easy in many situations to avoid an offender, practically speaking. Even if the victim tried not to have contact with the offender, the victim risks alerting others about what has happened. It is adaptive to "play nice" until prepared to deal with the full ramifications of leaving, reporting, or deciding to alert the offender of the problem.

Confusion and Disbelief About the Act and Actor

We have previously discussed the difficulty victims have in labeling an assault, rape, or beating as a crime. Even the term domestic violence somehow mitigates the acts of violence, protecting the perpetrator by failing to name the criminal. Labeling something a "domestic violence" incident does not call the abuser a criminal, nor does calling something "non-consensual sex." When examining how society is confused about violence and the perpetrators of violence, it is no wonder victims are easily confused. Non-consensual sex is rape; domestic violence is a perpetrator criminally assaulting a victim. Again, it is the relationship that confounds our definition and understanding of the crime. In particular, several studies indicate that when forced sex is perpetrated by a partner the victim is less likely to label that experience of forced sex as rape (Logan et al., 2015).

Remember, victims not only have to understand the act as a crime (rape, assault), they also have reorganize their understanding of the perpetrator. "My husband, a rapist? I could not wrap my head around that," a victim of marital rape said. "Never in a million years. It was only that last time that it really hit me, when I woke up choking on him." In her article in *The New York Times*, Salam (2018) quoted a rape victim who was drugged who said, "the feeling of 'what if I'm wrong?' made me panic more than 'what if I'm right?'" she said. "So I chose to believe that he didn't put anything in my drink. It was easier to believe him." Both of these victims could not define what had happened to them.

The offenders play into this confusion as well. "Dude last night didn't happen. Mee [sic] were both wasted. So we can never talk about it," a convicted offender texted to his male victim. After the victim responded, "you're lucky I don't kill you or report it," the offender texted, "okay man. You were in my bed with your dick out. Idk why." In a survey of my own offender clients, 60% stated that they produced confusion in their victims by "acting like nothing happened." Jeffrey Marsalis, a convicted serial rapist, would kiss his victims goodbye, bring them breakfast, or do other "normal" things to his victims to further confuse them. "I had a wonderful time last night. I hope you did too," he said to one (Erdely, 2008). She was already confused, since she had been drugged, but agreed to see him again.

Because these crimes are secretive and private, the victim sometimes only has the offender to help with the confusion. "What happened last night," one victim texted the offender. He responded, "what do you think happened. I'm so sorry I got the wrong message from you at the party. You told me to get in bed with you?" Another victim texted her boyfriend after being raped and strangled, "you hurt me. A lot. I am terrified to be around you." He responded, "don't try to turn this around on me though. I know I said things I didn't mean, but don't turn this around on me." "But you said you loved me. There is no way you loved me if you are capable of doing this to me," she responded. He replied, "I do and that's why I was so upset." A victim who feels so unloved and unvalued might be seeking comfort and assurance of her worth. "I was upset and confused. . . . I wanted to have a talk with him to try to understand why he would hit me, strangle me, and anally penetrate me without my consent," Emma Sulkowicz, another victim, explained about being assaulted by one of her closest friends (Zelinger, 2015). She contacted the man who raped her to find out why.

Wants to Be Normal and Safe Again

Remember the last time you experienced conflict with someone you had to be around? A coworker, in-law, lover, or friend? How relieved did you feel when the person acted fine again, when that awkwardness and tension left? Imagine this magnified by something so scary and awful like rape or physical abuse. Victims experience tremendous relief when they know they are safe again from the perpetrator. Victims strive to be normal again, to reject that they have been victimized, to avoid dealing with the aftermath, and to escape the feelings of vulnerability and loss of control.

Because assault is generally so private, the only person to offer them solace may be the offender. Another victim wrote an article, highlighting her shame about her behavior after her rape, "I asked him if he wanted to *stay*. To please sleep over. The request came out without thought, because I was so desperate to believe that our encounter had been consensual (Matis, 2018)."

Loves the Offender and Fears the Loss

Love is a powerful feeling. Many victims love their offender and feel loved back by the offender. There are times of peace and happiness in most ongoing relationships, even very abusive ones. Sometimes for victims, abuse or assault is simply the cost of the love. For example, women who experienced rape or forced sex in relationship accept it for the sake of preserving the relationship and out of fear of their partners leaving them (Valdovinos & Mechanic, 2017). Dan Reed, producer and director of *Leaving Neverland*, a documentary about Michael Jackson, captures this dynamic in a quote in *People* magazine. He says, "but I think once people understand that an abuser can be both your best friend, your mentor, and your idol and your lover, and that can happen while you're a child, and you never really disentangle those two things (Tracey & Green, 2019)."

It is important to understand how the offender evokes a focus on love and the fear of loss as well. They apologize, beg for forgiveness, promise to change, and portray the assault as a one-time thing. These behaviors make the victim feel terrible about holding the "mistake" against the offender. "We just had sex like so I'm confused. I'm sorry it happened like we shouldn't have done it. I heard everything. It's fine. I'll leave you alone and never speak to you again," texted one man who had raped his friend. Bonomi and colleagues captured this process in their study of prison phone calls, during which the offenders reminisced with the victims about their love and memories, the special places they visited, or their theme song (Bonomi, Gangamma, Locke, Katafiasz, & Martin, 2011). Another asked his battered wife, "I'm sorry. I want us to get better. I'm having a tough time communicating that. Would you consider counseling?" Later, he convinced her to recant, then sent her an article on borderline personality disorder to explain their volatility as a couple.

Thinks the Danger Can Be Controlled

If the victim is self-blaming or attributes the causes of the assault to something other than the offender's character or intention, the victim might think that the danger can be controlled, so does not see the need to avoid the offender. "I'll never be alone with him again," "I won't drink when we go out," or "I just won't start any trouble," are some examples of the way a victim might think that facilitates continued contact with the offender. Again, offenders perpetuate this kind of thinking, either attributing their behavior to the victims or citing an external source for their behavior. "If you only would have just . . ." is a common refrain of domestic violence offenders or child abusers who convince the victims that they are in control of the behaviors of the offenders. Making choices to change one's own behavior is far easier than facing the daunting task of leaving or reporting.

Danger

Victims of intimate violence face real danger when they stop contact with their abusers, even when not married to them. As discussed, they might experience retaliation, social rejection and isolation, or financial ruin. Offenders use the court system to drain the victim financially or can quit their jobs, file bankruptcy, or ruin the victims' credit. Children can be placed into foster care, away from their family. These are some of the real dangers, but the most real danger is death.

Leaving the offender can trigger a lethal response—not just for the victim, but for children and others as well. Domestic violence is the number-one risk factor in family annihilators (offenders who kill their whole family) and murder–suicides (Auchter, 2019). There is a high correlation between mass shootings and domestic violence, more than 50%, according to an analysis of the mass shootings between 2009–2017 (Everytown for Gun Safety, 2018).

Even if the victim does not face death, she faces the risk of other dangers. Stalking, an incredibly terrorizing and psychologically harmful behavior, occurs in a substantial portion of cases after victims have left an abusive partner, up to 58.5% in one study (Logan & Walker, 2010). Women who leave are raped and beaten. In Logan and Walker's study (2010), more than 89% of the women experienced severe physical violence after leaving, and more than 30% reported being raped. Stalking can occur over social media very easily as well. Victims must be cautious about who they are friends with, changing their relationship status, what they post, and privacy settings. Victims also face retaliation on social media as well, with offenders posting private pictures or engaging in other types of abuse online.

Abusers seek full custody of children more often than nonabusers and when they fight, they win more often (Bancroft, Silverman, & Ritchie, 2012). This produces the real danger of the loss of children to an abusive partner. It also creates the forum for the abuser to accuse the victim of false allegations, citing custody as a motive to lie or make the children lie. If the abuser is not given custody, there are other dangers. Abductions of children are most often committed by violent fathers in the context of domestic violence (Bancroft et al., 2012). In one study, no father abductor was punished, but 80% of the mother abductors were found and punished (Chesler, 2011). Children can also be used to stalk the victim, as custody agreements can require the victim to produce schedules of appointments and school activities, addresses, medical information, and more. Exchanges of children allow the offender contact with the victim. Children can provide private information, take things from the home for the offender, and facilitate the use of technology for stalking and harassment. An offender can give the child a phone, tablet, or laptop whose camera or GPS can be used to stalk the victim or record what happens in the home. Children face real risks when unsupervised with a violent parent and are at risk for more abuse, neglect, manipulation, or alienation from the victim (Bancroft et al., 2012).

Suggestions for Interviews

It is easy to magnify a victim's resistance to investigation and prosecution when addressing a relationship with the offender. From the outside, through the lens of investigation and prosecution, we are focused on the horrible assault and betrayal of the love and responsibilities of relationships. However, the victim might not be focused on these things by the time we are able to intervene. More likely, the victim is struggling with confusion, sadness, denial, and loss. The victim has the larger context of the relationship and the manipulations of the offender to place the event.

Sometimes, in fear, frustration, and helplessness, helpers of all types try to convince the victim that the offender is bad or evil. This is not likely to be the victim's total experience of the offender and can increase the victim's defense of the abuser and rejection of the helper. In fact, when a victim begins to feel aligned with an offender against a common enemy, their bond can become stronger (Bonomi et al., 2011).

Remember that the victim became attached to the offender for a reason. Explore those reasons with the victim. In fact, if the victim can get on the stand and talk about the positive feelings for the offender, it helps juries understand the attachment as well as dilutes any defense argument of hatred or vindictiveness in the victim. Some sample questions might be:

- What made you fall in love with him at first?
- What did you like about him?
- What things did she give you that made you go back?
- What it like when he wasn't abusing you?
- How did he convince you he had changed or wouldn't do it again?
- What things did you tell yourself to be able to keep loving him?

In Appendix A, I offer more questions for the exploration of these issues. In helping the victim understand the issue of the danger of the offender or why you are pursuing charges, I use the analogy of cancer—most of the body might be healthy, but the small percentage that is cancerous will kill you. This allows the victim to understand your role and perspective, while still respecting the attachment.

When you are interviewing the victim, use crime language to remind the victim that a crime was committed. Do not use the words "sex," "oral sex," or "sexual intercourse." Those are not crimes. Get used to saying things like "he put his mouth on your genitals" or "forced his penis into your vagina." This is imperative, not only to the victim, but to the judge and jury as well. Any mitigation of the act or label that softens the violence works against your case. Try to pair the actor with the action. For example, instead of saying "there was domestic violence in this relationship," say, "the defendant punched and strangled his wife on repeated occasions."

Summary

It is almost always safe to assume that you will have to understand the preexisting relationship between the offender and victim. You will always have to explore whether there was one. The relationship becomes a burden for the victim and benefits the offender for many reasons. Relationships are a primary factor impacting victim behavior. Remember:

- The offender relies on the relationship to succeed in repeatedly assaulting the victim, ensuring the victim's compliance and silence, and fostering protection from the victim.
- The relationship with the victim affords the offender the opportunity to manipulate others in the circle, exerting influence, establishing status, and dictating others' perception of the victim.
- The relationship can often camouflage the abuse or provide alternative explanations to the victim.
- The victim will struggle with disbelief and confusion, not only about the assault, but about the offender.
- In regard to why continued contact occurs, there are many things that facilitate continued contact, including:
  - Practical issues, like resources, children, location, and more;
  - A failure to accurately label an assault, negating the need to cease contact with an offender;
  - The need to feel normal, safe, and comforted;
  - Love and the fear of losing it;
  - A belief that the danger is over or can be controlled; and
  - Potentially deadly consequences for leaving.

Try to understand how the offender exploited and manipulated the relationship before, during, and after the assaults, then organize your case to expose this exploitation. Remind the juries or panels that loving is not a crime, hoping is not a crime, having a relationship is not a crime—what the offender did was a crime. Also, remember that it is not you against the victim, so align yourself with understanding their needs, then give other information that furthers the case.

As a relationship is used by the offender against the victim, you can establish a positive, supportive relationship with the victim that counters some of the offender impact. Understand the power of relationships. Begin at the beginning to foster a relationship that will sustain the victim and your case.

References

Antonova, N. (2017, October 13). Some victim stayed friends with Harvey Weinstein. I did the same with my rapist. Here's why. *Vox*. Retrieved from www.vox.com/first-person/2017/10/13/16465064/harvey-weinstein-rape-allegations-asia-argento

Auchter, B. (2019). Men who murder their families: What research tells us. *National Institute of Justice*. Retrieved from www.ncjrs.gov/pdffiles1/nij/230412.pdf

Bancroft, L., Silverman, J., & Ritchie, D. (2012). *The batterer as parent: Addressing the impact of domestic violence on family dynamics*. Los Angeles, CA: Sage.

Bonomi, A. E., Gangamma, R., Locke, C. R., Katafiasz, H., & Martin, D. (2011). "Meet me at the hill where we used to park": Interpersonal processes associated with victim recantation. *Social Science & Medicine, 73*, 1054–1061.

Chesler, P. (2011). *Mothers on trial: The battle for children and custody*. Chicago, IL: Lawrence Hill Books.

Connor, T. (2017, June 7). Bill Cosby sexual assault trial: Andrea Constand grilled over phone records. *NBC News*. Retrieved from www.nbcnews.com/storyline/bill-cosby-scandal/bill-cosby-sexual-assault-trial-andrea-constand-grilled-over-phone-n769296

Erdely, S. (2008, November). The crime against women that no one understands. *Self*. Retrieved from https://www.self.com/story/serial-rapist

Everytown For Gun Safety. (2018, December 6). *Mass shootings in the United States: 2009–2017*. Retrieved from https://everytownresearch.org/reports/mass-shootings-analysis/

Katz, C., & Barnetz, Z. (2016). Children's narratives of alleged child sexual abuse offender behavior and the manipulation process. *Psychology of Violence, 6*(2), 223–232. doi:10.1037/a0039023

Logan, T., & Walker, R. (2010). Toward a deeper understanding of the harms caused by partner stalking. *Violence and Victims, 25*(4), 440–455.

Logan, T., Walker, R., & Cole, J. (2015). Silent suffering and the need for better understanding of partner sexual violence. *Trauma, Violence, and Abuse, 16*, 111–135.

Matis, A. (2018, October 17). Continuing a relationship with a rapist doesn't mean it didn't happen. *Daily News*. Retrieved from www.nydailynews.com/opinion/ny-oped-rape-and-relationships-20181016-story.html

Policastro, C., & Payne, B., (2013). The blameworthy victim: Domestic violence myths and criminalization of victimhood. *Journal of Aggression, Maltreatment, & Trauma, 22*, 329–347. doi:10.1080/10926771.2013.775985

Salam, M. (2018, September 7). Victims of sexual violence often stay in touch their abusers. Here's why. *New York Times.* Retrieved from www.nytimes.com/2018/09/07/style/domestic-sexual-abuse-relationships-abuser.html

Tracey, B., & Green, M. (2019, March 1). Alleged Jackson victim admits he still feels protective of Michael: "I felt like I let him down". *People.* Retrieved from https://people.com/music/alleged-michael-jackson-victim-still-feels-protective-of-him/

Valdovinos, M., & Mechanic, M. B. (2017). Sexual coercion in marriage: Narrative accounts of Mexican-American women. *Journal of Ethnic & Culture Diversity in Social Work, 26*(4). doi:10.1080/15313204.2017.1300437

Zelinger, J. (2015, February 3). "The treatment of Emma Sulkowicz proves we have no idea how to talk about rape." *The Mic.* Retrieved from https://www.mic.com/articles/109446/the-treatment-of-emma-sulkowicz-proves-we-still-have-no-idea-how-to-talk-about-rape

Chapter 8

"Nah, I'm Good"
Understanding Victim Resistance

I hate myself. I should've punched him in his fucking face. I mean, I tried. He would ask me if I wanted 'play time' or 'a taste.' I would say, 'nah, I'm good.' Sometimes it would work. He would get pissed off and go away. Lots of times it wouldn't."
—Sam, a 15-year-old boy being abused by his adoptive father

Victim resistance, or lack thereof, often is a topic of interest to juries and defense attorneys, requiring exploration and explanation. As discussed earlier, there is a steadfast expectation held by jurors that victims will fight earnestly or vigorously to prevent being sexually assaulted (Ellison & Munro, 2009; Ellison & Munro, 2013). Historically, women were legally held responsible for resisting rape (Ullman, 2007). Male victims, too, face expectations of strength and to be "man enough" to resist assault (Walker, Archer, & Davies, 2005).

Because people understand the heinous and destructive nature of sexual assault, they anticipate a victim doing anything possible to resist being assaulted. When the victim does not, it is easy to turn that lack of resistance into doubt that the victim was "really" raped or assaulted. Implicitly, if she didn't fight, she might have consented. Or at least, the offender misunderstood the lack of consent.

When the victim is being sexually assaulted in a manner that fits the stereotype of rape, as in raped by a stranger, or with force or physical violence, the victim is more likely to respond with physical resistance. The victim might kick, yell, bite, or hit the assailant. The likelihood of strenuous resistance to assault increases when the characteristics of the assault fit rape myths. However, even in these assaults, violent physical resistance occurs the minority of the time (Ullman, 2007). Additionally, a number of studies show that the physical violence in rapes occur prior to the sexual assault, certainly impacting a victim's resistance during the assault itself (Scott & Beaman, 2004).

Most offenders, especially offenders of children, do not resort to physical violence during a sexual assault. In fact, they do not need to.

Coercion—verbal, physical, or both—is a highly successful way to complete an assault without causing serious injury or making a scene. In one study of college women who reported an unwanted or coerced sexual contact, in about half of the assaults, the offender used verbal tactics only (Edwards et al., 2014). More than 75% used verbal tactics and some physical coercion, like pinning the victim down or restraining the victim. None used overt violence like hitting, strangling, or battering. Stolzenberg and Lyon (2014) found in their study of closing arguments in acquittals of child sexual abuse that highlighting the offender's lack of force was successful for defense attorneys. Offenders will not use force when it is not necessary, unless force or violence is a source of arousal for them or if the violence serves another purpose. The use of overt force or violence by the offender makes it more likely that the victims will identify the assault as a rape or abuse and accurately label their experience (Kahn, Jackson, Kully, Badger, & Halvorsen, 2003). A more violent approach by an offender tends to lead to more victim resistance (Balemba, Beauregard, & Mieczkowski, 2012). This is not good for the offender.

So what impacts victim resistance? Why don't victims engage in behaviors that are likely to deter or prevent their sexual assault? First, it is important to understand and believe that victims almost always do resist, just not in the manner that our media-fueled expectations demand, even if the resistance is ineffective. "I used to tell him, 'dad, let's just watch the movie,'" she explained. "I would slide to the floor, off the couch, and I would try to get my sister to watch the movie with me." This young girl initially described herself as "just letting him do it" when talking about her father's sexual assault of her. But this wasn't true. The child attempted to redirect her father's attention, negotiate out of the abuse, and provide barriers that would prevent her abuser's actions. These are all types of resistance.

Let's Just Talk: Verbal Resistance

The victim's first line of defense is typically verbal. In fact, in an early study of more than 3,000 victims, 75% reported engaging in verbal resistance (Siegel, Sorenson, Golding, Burham, & Stein, 1989). This finding was replicated by Edwards and colleagues (2014). Most post-adolescent individuals have some practice at avoiding unwanted contact from others. We are socialized to subtly evade sexual advances, redirect undesired attention, and deter the progression of sexual attention without embarrassing or humiliating the other person. In early adolescence, most of us have memories of thoughtless and humiliating rejections. "Eeeew, gross," being laughed at, or being shoved away is something many of us have done or experienced. As we got older and understood the impact of that type of rejection, we learned more considerate diversions. We also learned

130 Common Types of Victim Responses

to be sensitive to those diversions, so as not to have to experience humiliating rejection as a recipient.

This generally happens before assault. The offender is likely to begin with verbal coercion, like begging, nagging, relentless pursuit, threats, or shaming the victim (Edwards et al., 2014). When the offender or the abuser begins the process of assaulting a victim, the victim typically responds verbally to that attempt. If the offender is not overtly violent, the victim will likely mirror the offender's behavior (Edwards et al., 2014; Ulman, 2007). The victim might say that she is "not into it," not comfortable, not ready, or attempt to play the attention off as a joke on the part of the offender. The victim might reference barriers, like the location or people in the next room, as an attempt to resist. The victim might even say the words "no," "stop," or "don't." When the offender does not respond to these cues, it is distressing or at least confusing for the victim. The behaviors that mean resistance in a typical sexual situation suddenly do not work for the victim in the situation with this offender. It's important to remember that human behavior falls back to what is familiar. When that familiar method does not work, the victim is left scrambling for new resources and coping.

Not only is the victim now faced with a situation that is growing alarming and confusing, he or she is now faced with an offender who is not responding in the expected way. The victim experiences confusion about the event, suddenly realizing that something is "not right," as well as understanding that she is with another person who's not following the rules and who is acting in an unanticipated manner. The victim now realizes that she is in a situation that is getting out of control.

There may be other signs of resistance that are verbal or nonverbal. A victim may bring up issues that seem surprising in an attempt to remind the offender of the potential consequences of behavior or to "snap them out of" the state the victim perceives the offender in. Some examples might include, "the children will hear," "I'm on my period," "I don't want to get pregnant," "do you have birth control," or other attempts to make the perpetrator pause or reconsider the choice to assault. Obviously, these statements can easily be used against the victim as "proof" of consent. This reflects the assumption that any conversation during a sexual assault again implies consent.

The victim may negotiate with the offender in an attempt to mitigate the damage or trauma. He might bargain or beg for one act in exchange for another, like begging the offender to "do anything but anal." In fact, the offender may offer the victim a "choice," like between oral versus vaginal penetration during the assault. "Yeah, I let him have it [vaginally]. I mean, anything is better than the last time he raped me. I bled [anally] for a few days," the wife of a rapist said about submitting when threatened. It is important to remember that when the victim makes a choice

"Understanding Victim Resistance" 131

offered by the offender, it is really not a choice. It's the offender's way of making the victim feel like she is cooperating, minimizing the appearance of coercion, and forcing the victim to participate. It is as much of a choice as a child has when asked, "would you rather be beaten with a stick or belt?" It is, however, a victim's way of having some minuscule amount of control in an uncontrollable situation.

Tie Them Really Tight: Nonverbal Resistance

Victims resist in other ways as well. The victim may turn her head, clench her mouth, try to hold her legs together, or refused to kiss the perpetrator. He might stare off into space and not respond at all, clearly indicating an unwillingness to participate. A victim pointed out, "I wouldn't kiss him or look at him. Tears were running down my face. Really? He thought that was consent?" This behavior is a clear and typically effective signal that the attention is unwanted in most normal sexual interactions. Imagine a consenting partner crying during intercourse, refusing to kiss or make eye contact, or lying frozen under a partner. A loving partner would become concerned and even perhaps lose the ability to be aroused in that situation. A rapist will not.

Other types of resistance might be more subtle, especially in victims of ongoing offenses. Children who are sexually abused might wear clothes to bed, try to lock their door, or try to have friends sleep over often. "I would tie my sweatpants really tight, hoping it would keep him from taking them off," said a woman being raped by her husband when she slept. "Or I would put ketchup on a pad in my underwear—he hated sex on my period." Others may try to repel the offender in various ways. "I would go days without showering, even getting teased at school," one victim explained. He said, "I would try to make myself as disgusting as possible, hoping if my dick was dirty, he wouldn't be interested." Sometimes this was effective for the victim; sometimes the offender forced the victim to shower. Gaining weight, tying pajama bottoms on tightly, or even behaving terribly to be punished are ways victims have discussed trying to resist the abuse. It is important to understand how and when and assaults occur to understand the victims' attempts to resist the offense. "He used to abuse me when we would go out for ice cream," the girl said. "I loved ice cream, but I would be real bratty so my mom wouldn't let me go." Getting in trouble and being punished is an effective resistance for abuse that occurs when your abusing grandpa takes you out for ice cream as a treat.

The same awareness is important in understanding the efforts of victims of domestic violence to avoid abuse. Victims engage in deflecting and placating behavior to calm and control the abuser. Sex might be one of these ways. Some victims attempt to distract the offender with sex to deescalate the offender or to escape assault. "I knew he would go to sleep after we had sex, so I would offer it to him when he began getting violent," one victim explained. Another, in an attempt to protect her child, said, "he started getting loud at the table. I could tell he was pissed off, so I took him in the bedroom." This particular example was used in court to "prove" that the victim was not afraid of the perpetrator. What no one asked her is what motivated that behavior. She would have explained that the abuser tended to throw hot, scalding things on her when he was angry. She was attempting to protect her baby, who was sitting at the breakfast table with them, from the perpetrator's hot coffee.

After an abusive episode, perpetrators often demand sex. This serves a number of functions for the perpetrator. A perpetrator might become aroused during a violent incident and needs to discharge that arousal. It might be a way to further dominate, possess, and oppress the victim, asserting himself sexually as he has physically and psychologically. "She needed to know she was mine, all of her," one abuser said. "I couldn't let her be and start thinking shit." It may be a distorted way of reconnecting after a violent incident; "make-up sex" that brings the victim relief and comfort that the abuse is over, as well as assures the offender that the victim is not going to report or cause a problem.

It is critical to remember that a victim's compliance with the sexual request from someone that is just harmed her is a nonconsensual act. It is a rare individual that would be sexually accessible to someone who has beaten, humiliated, or otherwise hurt him or her. However, it would be even more uncommon, even reckless, to refuse someone sexually who has just beaten or strangled you. The victim has just experienced the worst potential of their partner; she is unlikely to desire provoking that individual further through rejection.

Freeze, Flight, or Fight

Most people are familiar with the term "fight or flight" as a response to threat or danger. This term generally refers to our physiological response to perceived threat. However, it is incomplete. Physiologically, we experience three responses to threat and danger, appearing in this order: freeze, flight, or fight. These responses come from our limbic system, a deep and primitive brain structure that most animals possess. It is an automatic system that dictates instinctual coping mechanisms or responses to perceived danger.

Freeze

Freezing is how we respond first. When faced with danger, most animals will momentarily stop. Prey animals will remain frozen, assessing the danger and hoping to disinterest a predator. Since most predators are attracted by movement, freezing is an adaptive strategy to become invisible and unseen. Victims will often describe being frozen by fear, unable to choose or decide what to do next. This freezing may occur, making the victim feel helpless, temporarily, then turn into the victim's coping strategy. "I don't know why I didn't scream. I just felt frozen—I was terrified," she said. The victim went on, adding, "I mean, all I could think was 'what is happening?' Then it was too late, so I just laid there." Victims will often describe submitting to the assault because they felt overpowered, helpless, or so confused, choices were inaccessible. Some victims made a strategic choice to remain frozen so as not to antagonize the attacker or prolong the assault. This strategy is adaptive, considering that the victim is facing someone acting in a confusing, chaotic, unpredictable way. Victims do not expect to be attacked, so have no plan. "I just laid there and let it happen," the victim explained. "Then, after the first time, I realized it got over quicker that way anyway. Resisting only prolonged it, made it a fucking eternity."

The freeze response may become so extreme, it can result in a condition called tonic immobility. Tonic immobility is a state of involuntary system shutdown or paralysis in response to threat. It occurs in animals that freeze or play dead when attacked. It occurs in humans as well. The individual is literally physiologically frozen and unable to respond. Research suggests that up to 50% of rape victims experience this during a sexual assault (Campbell, 2012). This physiological response can last throughout an attack, even after for some time. Victims who have been previously assaulted as children are more at risk for this experience (Campbell, 2012). Unfortunately, although it is the body's way of attempting to survive a life-threatening event, it is associated with an extreme feeling of terror and helplessness, resulting in a higher incidence of PTSD in those who experience tonic immobility. Not only is sexual assault more likely to elicit tonic immobility than other types of trauma, but when it occurs, it is associated with a much poorer outcome for the victim's mental health, both male and female (Coxell & King, 2010; Campbell, 2012).

The freezing response is often misunderstood and held against victims. In a recent case of a convicted rapist whose case was overturned, the judges did not take the victims' freezing into account whatsoever. The article about the decision stated:

> Further, the appellate judges concluded that because of the noisiness of the survivor's bedding set-up, with their squad mates sleeping nearby, "it is hard to conclude beyond a reasonable doubt that appellant could complete the charged offenses without cooperation or detection."

> *The judges went on to write that they thought it was unlikely that the survivor wouldn't gasp or cry out when she woke up next to Whisenhunt, which would have alerted others to an assault.*
>
> —Myers, The Army Times, *June 4, 2019*

Flight

The second level of response requires more activity, the flight response. Attempted escape is expected of the victim if she is "really" being attacked. The victim is questioned about behaviors representing flight during or after the assault, like attempting to leave, texting or calling for help, getting out of the situation as soon as possible. These behaviors are judged. The absence of attempts to escape is something that is used to bring doubt on the victim's claims that a terrible or terrifying event has occurred.

First, is important to understand that escape or flight is a complicated issue involving much more than simply physically removing oneself from a situation. Explaining a failure to escape is easier for victims or investigators when there is no way to escape, like a child from a parent. When the reasons for failure to escape are evident in a case, they are unlikely to be questioned. It gets more complicated when routes of escape are deemed available by those assessing the case, as in the case of a college student who gets raped at a party or in a dorm or barracks room when her friends are next door.

In order to understand a victim's behavior regarding flight or escape, we must consider a number of things. It is possible that the victim did escape, but did so psychologically and not physically. Victims often cope with confusing or frightening situation by "checking out," or dissociating from the event. This is a psychological defense mechanism in which one simply psychologically leaves in order to minimize the experience of the event. A victim may describe feeling as if she's in a dream, feeling like it didn't happen, or like it was happening to a third person. The victim may describe the feeling that she was outside of her own body watching something happen. He might report an understanding that the assault was inevitable, so he just thought about other things. These are all forms of flight. "Oh," this adult male victim of sexual abuse by his father explained, "it began before the abuse. He would wink at me at the table—I knew what that meant. I started getting spacey right away."

Actual physical flight from a situation sounds so simple but is very complicated. It requires the assessment of many factors including resources, consequences, and a change in the situation. An attempt to leave or escape during an assault, or even after, might result in more serious consequences than the assault itself. An attempt to escape might evoke physical assault or backlash from the perpetrator. It might bring attention to the assault itself from outsiders who may not support the

"Understanding Victim Resistance" 135

victim or may pose a danger to victim; for example, running out of a party filled with the offender's friends. The victim may not be able to leave. For instance, the victim may have ridden with the perpetrator or third-party and not have had immediately available transportation. The victim might not know where he is or where to go. She may need to avoid attention because of fear or shame of what has occurred. Escape might entail leaving someone behind or exposing someone, like a child, to an event they need to be protected from. A woman I worked with, who was shot at by her husband in their home, was able to escape. However, the children were left in her home. Her husband took the children hostage, requiring a SWAT team to come rescue them.

Finally, after an assault, a victim may feel no more need to leave or escape. The worst is over. If the victim is familiar with the offender, she may know that after the assault there is period of calm or know that the danger is passed and escape is unnecessary. The victim might be exhausted from stress or terror, under the influence, or might simply believe that leaving was fruitless because the worst had happened. "I was so exhausted, I just fell right to sleep," she said. "He was already out, so what was the point? It was over."

Often, opportunities for escape are known after the assault is over. For instance, in one case I worked on, the offender left the victim for 20 minutes to go get a pizza. These 20 minutes were a significant focus of the defense as an opportunity to escape that the victim failed to take. Both sides forgot that this opportunity was only identified in hindsight. At the time, the victim had no idea how long the offender would be gone. Looking back, that time ended up being 20 minutes. But during the crime, the victim did not experience a 20-minute block of time. The victim experienced each minute as another minute of anticipation, wondering when the offender would be back, how long it would take a friend to get there, whether this was a test by the offender for the victim, and listening to each sound outside the door, vigilant for more abuse. It was only clear that she could have left or called someone after the time period was over.

Escape is not necessarily the primary issue on a victim's mind. Wanting the assault to be over is the primary focus of the victim. Attempts at escape create the possibility of provoking the offender, bringing attention to the assault, and worsening a bad situation. This should be considered when a victim falls asleep after an assault, goes to breakfast with the assailant, or publicly says goodbye in what appears to be a "normal" way. For victims of domestic violence, attempts at escape can escalate a situation dramatically, even fatally. Many victims are killed when attempting to escape or leave volatile relationships. For example, one victim I worked with was stabbed 27 times with a screwdriver by her husband as she walked out the door with their baby. He had been verbally and emotionally abusive before that, but, physically, had only pushed her years before.

The leaving triggered his rage. This same man took her hostage when she gave him divorce papers in the prison visiting room, dragging her into the guard office and trying to cut her throat with a shank. Each incident was defined by the perpetrator as her leaving him, something that made him extremely dangerous. For each victim, it is important to believe that all of their choices reflect the victim's best choice to maintain normalcy and safety, while attempting to ensure that nothing new happens. Victims have significant wisdom about the perpetrators they know.

Most importantly, flight is something we choose when we have identified danger and escape is viable. In a previous chapter we have already discussed that many victims fail to identify the danger they are in or what is happening. As noted, many victims do not identify their experience as rape or assault until after the event. They are in disbelief that the assault is occurring or that they need to escape an enemy. The offender is typically someone they want to be with, enjoy, and expect to act in accordance with friendship or love. The offender may not have been perceived as a threat to escape until the assault. And afterwards, the offender and his behavior might have returned to "normal," confusing the victim about what has happened and reassuring her that it won't happen again. For most people, running away is not a common or familiar behavior, but an extreme choice without alternatives against an identified enemy. "I didn't understand," she said. "He was my best friend. I didn't think he would ever hurt me. I just wanted to be friends again."

Fight

Identification of an enemy is important in the fight response. Although many people suggest that they would immediately react to threat with combat, this is not the case. Most victims of violent assault react protectively, not combatively. A child being hit covers his face. A woman being battered curls into herself to protect herself as much as possible. It is important to remember that "fighting" occurs between combatants— people mutually engaged in a violent act. A victim of a violent act is not a combatant, but a person trying to protect him- or herself in the face of a newly identified enemy. This enemy was not identified before the assault and perhaps not even during it. In fact, the confusion about the offender's behavior and intention keeps the victim from recognizing the offender as a danger. He is simply "drunk," "angry," "pushy," or a mystery. Rarely, except in extreme circumstances, do victims think, "I better fight for my life or this guy is going to kill me." Victims, especially of domestic violence, are likely to think, "he is going to kill me" or "I am going to die tonight." However, fighting against the attacker in a way different from that already attempted (pushing, scratching, squirming), is unlikely to be a consideration or an option during the crisis.

This is even more true during a sexual assault. Even in a study focused solely on convicted rapes of victims by strangers, only 17% engaged in active physical violence, mainly kicking, during the rape (Woodhams, Hollin, Bull, & Cooke, 2012). The violent response itself only occurred after the victim realized that rape was the assailant's intent and the rape was in process. Before and during the assault, victims respond in a variety of ways to resist nonviolently, like struggling, negotiating, crying, or other more passive attempts. As noted, fighting has to be an active decision by the victim. If the victim does not realize she is being sexually assaulted, is confused or in shock, or fears for her safety, she will not vigorously resist.

Not only might the victim not choose to fight, she might choose not to fight. The victim might fear provoking the attacker or prolonging the assault. She might fear genital or other injury through fighting. At the time, a choice to fight becomes clear to the victim or necessary, the victim might have decided that resistance was futile. Male victims carry a significant expectation that they will resist assault and be successful at it (Tewksbury, 2007). Remember, survival is the victim's primary focus.

Barriers to Resistance

There are many things that contribute to a victim's decision not to resist. These factors can be uncontrollable reactions or conscious decisions that the victim makes about responding.

Children or Protection of Others

Sometimes victim resistance involves alerting others to the assault or endangering others during the assault. Often these others are children. A mother being raped by her husband may face a very difficult choice regarding resistance if she fears her children will be awakened and perhaps witness the assault. Children are often a barrier to resistance or escape. Not only will the parent not want to expose the child to the violence but also may fear that the attacker will harm the children directly. "Oh really? I was supposed to yell and scream? And what?" asked a victim after being confronted about not screaming during a rape by her estranged husband. "Wake the grandkids up and have them see Pop-pop raping Nana?"

The victim may choose to protect others as well. Family members who are witness to domestic violence assaults might face danger from the perpetrator. The perpetrator may have threatened other potential witnesses or helpers or have shown the capacity to harm others. One victim of partner violence I worked with saw her father beaten up by her husband when attempting to help her leave. Another saw her mother pushed to the floor when she tried to get between the victim and her attacker.

138 Common Types of Victim Responses

Protection of others might include protection from a direct physical threat, but also might include emotional or social protection. The victim may not want to expose the other person to involvement. "I was terrified about it ending up in the paper," said a woman about her husband's abuse. "I mean, my kids go to school. Their name might not be in the paper, but their dad's is." Imagine the feelings of the child and parent who had to face the school project about genealogy and googling the child's last name, only to find headline after headline about their father's violence and sexual offense. The victim might want to protect him- or herself from the scrutiny of others. In trial, this can go far beyond the event, like an exploration of motive to fabricate. A recent victim in a trial had each credit card balance displayed publicly to show she that had a financial motive to lie. Crying out for help-seeking during a sexual assault exposes the victim to very basic issues of sexual privacy; being seen naked, feeling judged or humiliated; or, again, inciting the offender. If the victim is experiencing shame or feelings of responsibility for the attack, she may have not decided to even tell anyone about it, never mind seek help for it. The victim is experiencing a situation beyond their control. Adding others to that situation releases more control, something a victim may not be prepared to do.

Prior History of Abuse

The victim's prior history of victimization can be a strong influence on a decision to resist. Past experience may have taught the victim that resistance is futile, brings about greater harm, or prolongs the assault. Depending on the nature of the prior victimization, the victim's past learning might confuse the victim more about the nature of the offense. I already described the child who been sexually abused throughout her therapy by her foster father, a man she described as playful and gentle. He sexually abused to her through seduction, gifts, and exposure to pornography. As a child, she could not associate this with the abuse we talked about in therapy. She had access to all the help possible, but couldn't choose to escape or seek help because of her confusion, leading to her revictimization. Another boy I treated was brutally anally raped by his grandfather. When a friend of the family, a much older man (50s), seduced the teenager (13), he experienced sexual pleasure and thought they were "in love." A prior history of abuse is associated with a decreased likelihood of overt resistance to assault, especially in a relationship with the perpetrator (Norris et al., 2006). It is also associated with tonic immobility or other defenses, like dissociation, that were previously relied upon by the victim (APA, 2013; Campbell, 2012)

Inability to Resist

A victim's resistance might be predicated on that victim's ability to resist physically. A child is unlikely to engage in resistance against an adult.

A victim might be overpowered physically by the assailant. Decreased resistance is associated with victim intoxication as well (Scott & Beaman, 2004; Norris et al., 2006). Obviously, a drugged or seriously intoxicated victim will not have a great ability to resist effectively, especially if that victim is in and out of consciousness. Offenders of children will target the victims at times when they are vulnerable, especially when the victims are sleeping. Again, a sleeping victim cannot resist an assault. If the victim is elderly, infirm, or otherwise incapacitated, resistance is not possible. An offender I evaluated engaged in the rapes of women in comas. Another sexually assaulted women with dementia. These offenders specifically chose victims who could not resist. The disabled victim is highly vulnerable to abuse.

There are cognitive and psychological issues that make a victim unable to resist. The cognitive limitations of a victim with intellectual disabilities could hamper that victim's ability to understand what is happening. Compliance does not necessarily mean consent to a victim who does not understand or who might not have been educated about sex, sexuality, or consent. Resistance may not have been a consideration for the victim. A victim who is always in the care of others, like an individual with disabilities, might be socialized to comply with whatever physical demands the caretaker makes. These individuals could have issues with communication as well.

Summary

The issue of resistance is a complex one. Although victims are expected to physically resist assault, their resistance can be used against them. When a victim was portrayed as resisting "too much" while being assaulted by an acquaintance, the study participants felt sympathy for the rapist (Branscomb & Weir, 1992). The term "mutual combat" is used against victims of intimate partner assault who fight back or try to defend themselves. The dynamics of resistance are complex and require exploration by investigators. Some points to remember are:

- An educated investigator or prosecutor will look for avenues of resistance or reasons the victim did not resist in a stereotypical way. Looking for the victim's resistance is a different process than simply focusing on the absence of physical violence, screaming, or attempts to escape an assault situation.
- There are three responses to threat: freeze, flight, and fight. Victims engage in all of these behaviors. A good interview will reveal this.
- There are other barriers to resistance, including:
  - Fear;
  - Protection of children or witnesses;

- Prior history of abuse; and
- Inability to resist.

- Not only will looking for the victim's resistance help your case, it will help the victim. Victims who believe they did not resist suffer more significant issues of self-blame, shame, and guilt, as well as are more likely to have more severe mental health symptoms following the assault.
- There are legally defined expectations for the strength and type of victim resistance that differ by jurisdictions. Be familiar with what is required for you and how to present the victims' resistance at trial.

References

American Psychiatric Association. (2013). *Diagnostic and statistical manual of mental disorders* (5th ed.). Arlington, VA: American Psychiatric Association.

Balemba, S., Beauregard, E., & Mieczkowski, T. (2012). To resist or not to resist? The effect of context and crime characteristics on sex offenders' reaction to victim resistance. *Crime & Delinquency, 58*(4), 588–611. doi:10.1177/0011128712437914

Branscombe, N., & Weir, J. (1992). Resistance as stereotype-inconsistency: Consequences for judgment of rape victims. *Journal of Social and Clinical Psychology, 11*(1), 80–102. doi:10.1521/jscp.1992.11.1.80

Campbell, R. (2012, December 3). The neurobiology of sexual assault. *An NIJ Research for the Real World Seminar*. National Institute of Justice: US Department of Justice. Retrieved from www.nij.gov/multimedia/presenter/presenter-campbell/Pages/welcome.aspx

Coxell, A., & King, M. (2010). Adult male rape and sexual assault: Prevalence, revictimization, and the tonic immobility response. *Sexual and Relationship Therapy, 25*(4), 372–379. doi:10.1080/14681991003747430

Edwards, K., Probst, D., Tansill, E., Dixon, K., Bennett, S., & Gidycz, C. (2014). In their own words: A content-analytic study of college women's resistance to sexual assault. *Journal of Interpersonal Violence, 29*(14), 2527–2547. doi:10.1177/0886260513520470

Ellison, L., & Munro, V. (2009). Reacting to rape: Mock jurors' assessments of complainant credibility. *British Journal of Criminology, 49*, 202–219. doi:10.1093/bjc/azn077

Ellison, L., & Munro, V. (2013). Better the devil you know? "Real rape" stereotypes and the relevance of a previous relationship in (mock) juror deliberations. *The International Journal of Evidence & Proof, 17*, 299–322. doi:10.1350/ijep.2013.17.4.433

Kahn, A., Jackson, J., Kully, C., Badger, K., & Halvorsen (2003). Calling it rape: Differences in experiences of women who do or do not label their sexual assault as rape. *Psychology of Women Quarterly, 27*, 233–242. doi:10.1111/1471-6402.00103

Myers, M. (2019, June 4). A West Point cadet just had his rape conviction overturned, leaving him free to return to school. *The Army Times*. Retrieved from www.armytimes.com/news/your-army/2019/06/04/a-west-point-cadet-just-had-his-rape-conviction-overturned-leaving-him-free-to-return-to-the-school/

Norris, J., George, W. H., Stoner, S. A., Masters, N. T., Zawacki, T., & Davis, K. C. (2006). Women's responses to sexual aggression: The effects of childhood trauma, alcohol, and prior relationship. *Experimental & Clinical Psychopharmacology, 14*(3), 402–411.

Scott, H., & Beaman, R. (2004). Demographic and situational factors affecting injury, resistance, completion, and charges brought in sexual assault cases: What is best for arrest? *Violence and Victims, 19*(4), 479–495.

Siegel, J., Sorenson, S., Golding, J., Burham, M. A., & Stein, J. (1989). Resistance to sexual assault: Who resists and what happens? *American Journal of Public Health, 79,* 27–31.

Stolzenberg, S., & Lyon, T. (2014). Evidence Summarized in attorney's closing arguments predicts acquittals in criminal trials of child sexual abuse. *Child Maltreatment, 19*(2), 119–129. doi:10.1177/107755951453988

Tewksbury, R. (2007). Effects of sexual assaults on men: Physical, mental, and sexual consequences. *International Journal of Men's Health, 6*(1), 22–35. doi:10.3149/jmh.0601.22

Ullman, S. (2007). Relationship to perpetrator, disclosure, social reactions, and PTSD symptoms in child sexual abuse survivors, *Journal of Child Sexual Abuse, 16*(1), 19–36. doi:10.1300/J070v16n01_02

Walker, J., Archer, J., & Davies, M. (2005). Effects of rape on men: A descriptive analysis. *Archives of Sexual Behavior, 34*(1), 69–80. doi:10.1007/s10508-005-1001-0

Woodhams, J., Hollin, C., Bull, R., & Cooke, C. (2012). Behavior displayed by female victims during rapes committed by lone and multiple perpetrators. *Psychology, Public Policy, and Law, 18*(3), 415–452.

Chapter 9

"Commit to Courage"
Conclusions and Suggestions

The world is a dangerous place to live, not because of the people who are evil, but because of the people who don't do anything about it.
—*Albert Einstein*

Prosecution of intimate violence is challenging, frustrating, exciting, and heartbreaking. It is some of the most important work you will ever do. Interpersonal violence is a contamination of the very things that make us the most human. Offenders weaponize the qualities of love, hope, and trust, making them frailties instead of strengths. You are in a unique position to stop this. Hopefully, reading this book has made you feel more prepared to confront some of the issues.

In the scores of trials I have observed, I can say that one of the biggest pitfalls in these trials of sexual assault or intimate violence is the seduction of defending the victim instead of prosecuting the offender. Because defense tactics almost exclusively focus on denigrating and discrediting the victim and because trials often hinge on the credibility of the victim, the case can easily turn into a trial about the victim, the victim's behaviors, and the victim's character. This can become so entrenched in the case that all witnesses revolve around the victim, all rebuttal is about the victim, much of the investigation can be focused on corroborating the victim, and the closing becomes about the victim. Interestingly, the media can co-opt this focus, highlighting defense issues about the victim while downplaying the evidence against the offender.

Almost without exception, the defense in these cases comprises mainly of adopting and promoting rape myths, misinformation about abuse, faulty expectations of victim response, and presentation of "evidence" that superficially seems to represent "common sense," but actually distorts it. For example, the expectation that human beings will and can automatically stop loving or being involved with someone who has hurt them is often presented with the following attitude: "of course, if this *really* happened, the victim would" stop loving, run, be afraid, have no

"Commit to Courage" 143

contact with, let go of, cut off, or otherwise be through immediately with the offender. In one trial, defense counsel asked a witness who was with a victim after the rape, "well, did she look like someone who was texting her rapist?" The right answer was, "yes, it looks just like that."

So what happens next? How do you take this information and make it work for you? Here's what I have found helpful for investigators and prosecutors.

- **Commit to courage**—In many offices, the pursuit of challenging cases is not encouraged, from the law enforcement who might be cynical about things changing to prosecutors who are burnt out, frustrated, or defeated. Commit to taking on these cases despite pushback or negative messages from others. Bring your passion to the work place. Remember, there are no bad facts, just challenges in these cases.
- **Reframe "winning"**—Winning is not just about disposing of a case or getting a conviction. Winning is about trying, learning, and support-ing victims. Even the most reluctant victim will respond to supportive efforts, increasing a willingness to come forward again or complete a prosecution. Offenders are also exposed by efforts; an acquittal builds a record that will surely matter next time.
- **Be offender-focused in your case**—In the theory, theme, opening, questioning, and closing, focus on the offender's behaviors and deci-sions, as well as the offender's influence on the victim and witnesses. Get at the offender's intentions, what the offender did to facilitate or exploit the situations. It is not "how much did you drink" to the victim, it is "how many drinks did he buy you after you were already intoxicated?" If the offender is a "nice guy," show how he used being nice to fool people and gain access to the victims.
- **Educate the judge and jury**—Beginning at voir dire, you have an opportunity to address the biases and misinformation in your jury or panel. Do it through the way you ask questions, through the victim, and in your argument.
- **Use expert witnesses**—Consider using an expert. Medical experts can address injury or lack of injury, especially in strangulation cases. Victim behavior experts or psychologists can help explain victim response, trauma, memory, disclosure, or many other issues that are subject to misinformation.
- **Address the issues directly**—Prepare the victim to answer the ques-tions you fear the jury will have. Be ready to address motives, lies, inconsistencies, or challenging facts straight on with the witnesses.
- **Avoid "why" questions with victims**—"Why" is a very blaming ques-tion. It gives the message that an expectation has been violated. For example, "why didn't you leave?" highlights the expectation that the victim should have left. "What made you stay?" does not give the

jury the same message that the victim did something wrong. Learn how to ask questions differently than asking "why," remembering that every "why" question blames. Examples of these are offered in Appendix A. On the other hand, "why" questions can be very effective at pointing out the decisions of the offender. "Why would you separate her from her friends?" "Why would you give her more to drink when you could see she was drunk?" These types of questions reveal the poor choices of the offender.

- **Learn evidence-based investigation and prosecution**—From the beginning of a report, you are afforded an opportunity to collect evidence that might not be available later. Outcry evidence, statements from victims, children, and witnesses, text messages, photos, or anything that substantiates the report should be gathered in the event that the victim chooses not to participate later.

- **Become more educated**—This book, while hopefully helpful, is an overview of many issues that are confronted in these trials, not a full education of all of them. Talk to your advocates and local resources. Read some books on intimate partner violence, offenders, sexual assault, and interviewing techniques. Watch and learn from your experts. Use your colleagues and professional organizations.

- **Self-care**—These cases are traumatic and can contribute to burn-out and compassion fatigue. You can become angry with victims, in part to combat your fear and helplessness when they return to a dangerous offender. You can become callous. Take care of yourself. Get a support system that understands your drive. And be honest with yourself—if you can't care anymore, don't get these cases.

- **Consider creative charging**—Sometimes your case might go south. Sometimes the perpetrator will manipulate your victim or witnesses. Do not be short-sighted by focusing only on the assault. Oftentimes, there are other crimes committed in the context of the sexual or physical assault or committed post-assault. Violations of protective orders are chargeable. Witness tampering, witness intimidation, or obstruction charges could be filed when an offender influences the victim. Trespass, property destruction, and other similar charges could be considered. Child endangerment or abuse charges could be filed against an offender if a child is present during an assault; if not, the offender should be reported to child protection agencies. Though some of these charges might seem minor, they might result in some type of supervision of the offender that will help protect the victim. The offender will also be in the system, which counts.

Remember, there is no perfect victim (follow #TheresNoPerfectVictim for more examples). If there is anything I sincerely hope you can remember and internalize, it is the understanding that the victim did not have a

"Commit to Courage" 145

crystal ball. The victim did not make choices with the knowledge that being raped or beaten would be the outcome of a decision, *even if it has happened before with the same offender*. Offenders are inconsistent, unpredictable, and variable. Their influence and power cannot be underestimated.

This is so hard for people to understand and accept. There is so much resistance to the idea that victims are not responsible for being raped or hurt. Victim blaming is so easy. Here are my thoughts about some of the opposition I and my colleagues have encountered and combatted, in and out of the courtroom:

- "What did she think was going to happen?"—That she would have a hangover, get grounded for sneaking out, have a good time, have a good marriage—not that she would be raped or beaten.
- "But those clothes she was wearing—like an advertisement"—Yes, an advertisement of sexual attractiveness; a wish for attention, perhaps, or meeting the style of dress, not an invitation to be raped. Not one offender I have ever treated chose to rape a woman because of the sexy clothes she was wearing.
- "She poked the bear, what did she think?"—No one pokes a bear because they can see it is a bear. The same with swimming with sharks. Or flashing money in a bad neighborhood. This concept is only relevant if you truly understand your situation—most victims DO NOT.

All of these examples, and more, have been used to try to prove the victim knew she was going to be assaulted or the man knew he was going to be raped, therefore they are responsible. Until the people who beat and rape others carry signs announcing their intention to do so, no victim ever makes their choice with the knowledge that they will be hurt going forward.

Finally, it is the offenders' behavior that is "counterintuitive," not the victims'. When someone violates the rules of the community and safety of others, follows brutality with kindness, pretends that nothing happened after a serious event, uses niceness as a weapon, and forms attachments just to exploit them, that is against all common sense and decency. Victims' behaviors and decisions are understandable human responses to the inexplicable behaviors of others, adaptive in an abnormal situation. When we can believe that, we can be better at holding offenders accountable.

Appendix A

Questions Instead of "Why?"

It is very difficult to elicit information from victims about their behavior or the decisions they made during and after an assault. When asked "why" questions, they can get defensive or simply respond "I don't know," because they have been asking themselves the same thing and no answer is good enough. The recent interview techniques that draw out the victim's internal experience, like "what was going on in your mind" or "how were you feeling then," have added a much richer level of information, but are also limited. For a panel or jury, I think that we rely on the jury to make the leap from "I was terrified" to "I didn't yell" on their own. Also, I believe that we completely miss the offender's influence on the victim's behavior and miss exposing that to the jury, panel, or judge.

Here are some suggestions for additional questions to ask victims, both in interviewing and on direct, that might be useful or informative. I have not broken them down into categories; the form of the questions can be used for most topics. What I hope to elicit in my questions are the decisions, choices, and strategies the victims use to make it through the attack, as well as the offender's behavior that influences the victim. In ongoing relationships with the perpetrator, there is a level of "training" of the victim that primes the response to the assault in question. You can try to get at this pattern, too. I believe in reassuring the victim that "everything makes sense when you understand it" and to encourage them to share even the most embarrassing things.

Questions

Forming the basic question without asking why can be difficult. Consider using these to start your questions:

- How did you decide to . . .
- What made you . . .
- What was going through your mind when . . .
- What were you thinking when . . .

Appendix A   147

- What did the offender do to . . .
- What were you feeling when . . .
- What was it like when . . .
- Tell me about when/what/how . . .

Victim Decision-Making and Experiences

- What made you decide not to [scream, leave, run]?
- When did you decide that it was okay to stay or that the danger was over?
- When did you believe it was safe? What made you think that?
- How did you decide [not to fight/not to scream/that it was safe/to go back to him?
- At the time this was happening, in the beginning, what did you think was going to happen or was happening?
- You [told him you loved him/sent him photos/sent him texts/had sex with him after]. What made you choose to do that?
- What made you think that [kissing him/having sex/not screaming] was a good idea at the time?
- How did you try to resist? Had this worked for you in the past with people?
- What did your past experience with abuse teach you about [resisting, coping, living with the offender]?
- How do your choices fit with your personality or who you believe you are? (*I am not violent, I wanted to stay to protect my friend, I don't like causing problems, I am a Christian/forgiving/taught to give people a second chance.*)
- What have you done to try to deal with this relationship in the past?
- What choices did you make during or after the assault to stay safe or deal with it?
- What decisions did you make to try to deal with him?
- Were there any things you thought were weird to think about at the time? (*Getting pregnant, or what would happen to your kids.*)
- Did anything strange happen to you, like leaving your body or something else?
- How did you try to help it be over?
- How did you cope when it was happening? How about after it was over?
- What questions do you think people have about how you acted?
- Do you blame yourself? How come?
- What have you learned from your family on how to deal with these things? Your religion? Your culture? The offender?
- How do you think other people will view this? Did this affect your decisions in any way?

148 Appendix A

- What was it like when it was good with [the offender]? How did it change?
- What things kept you from leaving?
- Have you ever tried to [leave/resist] before? What happened?

Offender Behavior

- How did you decide to forgive him?
- How did he help you get over it? Forgive him?
- What did he do to get you to come back? Trust him again?
- [What did he do/how did he act] after the assault? How did that affect you?
- How did he keep you quiet?
- What did he do to make you trust him?
- You [told him you loved him/sent him photos/sent him texts/had sex with him after]. What made you choose to do that? What did he do that helped you make that decision?
- What experience do you have trying to resist or fight with him? What does he do?
- What would usually happen between you after an assault?
- Before he raped you, did you have any reason to think he would do something like this?
- Tell me about the first time he did something you had to forgive or forget. How did he make it up to you? Blame you for it?
- What did he say to make you think this was your fault? How about before this? What did he say to make you think you brought stuff on yourself? (*Pushed my buttons, make me jealous, you know how I am, you are crazy.*)
- What has he done when you have tried to [leave/break up] before?
- What does he done to make you feel helpless?
- Has there ever been anything you could do to calm him down or make things good again? (*Pleasing, make-up sex, pretending it didn't happen.*) If you did these things, how did it get better for you?
- Has he ever said people wouldn't believe you or otherwise made you doubt your support? Has he proven it to you?
- How has he threatened or intimidated you in the past?
- What did he do during the time before the assault to make you feel safe? Confuse you? Isolate you? Increase your [vulnerability/intoxication]?
- What does he know about you that he has used against you?
- Are there ways he has threatened, intimidated, or controlled you?
- Does he know things about you that he hurts you with or that you are afraid others will find out?
- How does he act around other people? Does your family like him?
- Is it hard to believe he would do something like this? How come?

Appendix A   149

- Has he ever turned others against you? How has he done that?
- Does he ever use the children against you? Tell me about that.
- What will he be telling others about you? Is there something he is saying to his attorney about you or that event that we should know?

These questions will be a start in learning how to restructure how you can ask even the most difficult question. Remember, your questions convey the beliefs and attitudes that you will want the victim and your jury to have. Ask out of curiosity and don't avoid the difficult things. If a victim is able to present any issue openly, not only will it defuse any attack, but it will undermine any perception that the victim or prosecutor is hiding something important to the case. These questions can bring a victim's experience to life for the jury or panel, as well as reveal the offender.

Appendix B

Sample Voir Dire Questions

Voir dire is an important place to begin addressing myths, biases, and misinformation about intimate violence. Below are some sample areas to consider formulating questions around to address with your jury or panels. As I am not an attorney, I am not advocating for the specific format or content of these questions, as some might not be allowed. Rules of voir dire differ depending on the judge or jurisdiction in which you practice. Consider the content area for what you can personally address in your own courtroom.

Victim Behavior

Children

- Children keep secrets.
- Children don't have all the words to tell about things they don't know about.
- Children can love the people that abuse them.
- Children protect adults and don't want to get people in trouble.
- Children can be tricked by adults.
- Children might not have the ability to tell everything at once.
- Children's memories are different than adults.
- Victims can tolerate a lot of abuse out of fear, love, or just thinking it's normal.

Disclosure

- People don't like to think about or talk about embarrassing or private things, especially sex.
- Someone might remember different things at different times.
- Who asks the questions might affect how someone tells.
- Someone might not be ready to report abuse right away.
- A spouse might want to try to work on a marriage, even if the other spouse is abusive.

Appendix B   151

- People keep their sex lives private.
- It is hard to talk about sexual or embarrassing things to strangers.
- That just because someone doesn't say something exactly the same way every time it doesn't mean they are lying.
- People don't like to admit things they think makes them look like they "deserved" being hurt.
- Sometimes telling about abuse takes a long time, even years.
- Victims can deny or suppress their memories or belief about abuse.

Staying in an Abusive Relationship

- People can be terrified of being abandoned, poor, or family-less.
- Sometimes parents put their own needs above their children's.
- Sometimes it is easier to deny than to face abuse.
- People try to handle their problems by "keeping them in the family."
- It is really hard to leave someone you love.
- Someone can hope someone will change, especially if that person promises to change.
- Being dependent on someone can really impact how you deal with abuse from that person.
- Mothers think they can protect their children without telling about the abuse.
- People can be convinced there is "nothing you can do" about abuse.
- People can take marriage vows very seriously and be influenced by religion or culture.
- A victim can come to believe that sexual assault is just part of the relationship or "just how it is," especially if their sexual experience is limited.
- In relationships or when someone wants a relationship, can the person overlook serious flaws, faults, or behavior of the intended partner.

Triggers for or Factors Impacting Reporting

- Personalities and previous history can affect how people handle abuse or stress.
- Victims are more likely to tell when they have support and resources.
- Victims who are isolated are not likely to tell.
- Victims who have no place safe to go or don't know what to do won't tell.
- Sometimes an event or change will compel someone to do something about abuse.
- People can be threatened into silence.
- People can have a belief about someone that is very hard change regardless of that person's behavior—like if people think someone is a nice guy.

152 Appendix B

- Culture be a strong influence on how someone deals with a sexual assault.
- A victim can fail to identify sexual assault or abuse by a sexual or intimate partner, maybe thinking that the partner just "lost control" or was stressed out.

Offender Behavior

- Sexual assault is a secret crime.
- Offenders can manipulate and trick the victims.
- Sexual abuse is so unbelievable people chose to deny it.
- Offenders commit crimes in private, with no witnesses.
- Abusers can often promise to never do it again to reassure people they are safe.
- Offenders exploit people's vulnerability to get access to victims.
- Offenders can play on people's sympathy so they don't get in trouble.
- Offenders can be really nice to people as well as assault them.
- Offenders can be good at their jobs or good in public and still hurt people.
- Offenders can be very adept at getting people dependent on them.
- Offenders take advantage of people's shame, embarrassment, and fear.
- Offenders are often liked and valued by the people around them.
- Offenders can hide their abuse in "normal" behavior, like horseplay.
- Offenders make promises that they break.
- There is no physical evidence related to being kissed, touched, rubbed, licked, tickled, or having to watch things.
- Offenders intimidate or threaten victims into silence.
- Offenders should be held accountable for their own choice to abuse.
- Offenders should be held accountable even if someone "lets" them abuse or goes back.
- Offenders should be held accountable even if someone "doesn't tell."
- Offenders should be held accountable even if another parent "doesn't protect" the victims.
- Offenders use many excuses for sexually assaulting people.
- Alcohol does not cause you to be sexually attracted to children.
- Depression does not cause people to be sexually attracted to children.
- Offenders exploit their rank, status, or power to facilitate their assaultive behavior.
- Offenders use tools, like rank or alcohol, to get away with rape.
- A mother is not responsible for an offender's behavior of sexually abusing kids.
- A mother cannot cause someone to sexually assault their kids.
- A mother might fail to protect children without being responsible for the offender's behavior.

Appendix B   153

- A child cannot make an adult sexually abuse them.
- A woman cannot make someone rape them.
- You cannot tell who a rapist or abuser is by the way they look.

Review some of the information throughout the book, especially the myths and biases that juries maintain about intimate violence, victims, and offenders. Good voir dire questions can educate the jury at the onset of the trial, as well as help choose jurors who are the least biased or misinformed about these very difficult issues.

Appendix C

Interviewing Victims for Sentencing

In order to capture the full impact of a rape/sexual assault on a victim, you have to think of the effects as radiating or rippling. The victim is more than a victim—he or she is a person, partner, parent, community member, and more who has been impacted in the micro- and macrocosm of his or her world. To capture all the facets of the impact, I have created a set of questions that might help you assess the consequences on multiple levels of the victim's experience. Sometimes, it is useful to structure the interview from micro to macro. Here are some thoughts:

1. **Self**—Probe the impact on the person's individual identity.

    a. How did this affect how you feel about yourself?
    b. What are some of the symptoms you struggle with now?

        i. Sleep problems
        ii. Anxiety, depression, irritability
        iii. Loss of joy
        iv. Social withdrawal
        v. Nightmares, hypervigilance, hyperarousal
        vi. Appetite problems
        vii. Emotional numbing
        viii. Efforts to avoid all reminders, triggers, places
        ix. Concentration, attention, learning disruption

    c. Look for themes of shame, guilt, blame, helplessness, disempowerment
    d. Also, look for themes of damaged, ruined, dirty
    e. "Now I need meds/treatment"—mentally ill, "sick"
    f. How has this affected your sense of self-worth? Lovability? Sense of value?
    g. Physical health or injury from the assault

2. **Woman/Man/Gender Identity**—explore changes in sense of self as a sexual being or gender identity.

Appendix C   155

a. Did this affect your sexuality?
b. Do you have any feelings of disgust or shame about sex? Your body?
c. Did it make you feel differently about being [gender identity]? (Weak, helpless)

3. **Partner/Lover/Parent**—explore changes in intimate relationships.

a. How did this affect your relationship with your lover/spouse?
b. Has it affected your sex life?
c. Has it affected your trust in your lover? Your ability to be intimate? Share feelings?
d. Can you be vulnerable in your relationships?
e. Are your habits with your family changed? (Don't go out, don't sleep with, overprotective of the children, won't go places with the family)
f. Do you have issues with depression, anger, irritability that impact your family?
g. Have you lost your sense of competency or desirability as a mate?
h. Are some of your trauma symptoms drawing you away from others? (Not able to be hugged by children)
i. How has this affected your parenting or bond with your children?
j. How has this impacted the dynamics in your family?

4. **Person/Community/Friend/Family/Work**

a. Has this rape/assault changed the way you interact with others?
b. Is it as easy to be someone's friend?
c. Can you trust people as easily?
d. Did you get support from others?
e. Did you withdraw? Did you lose friends from this?
f. Has this changed the way you deal with strangers?
g. Are you different when you are around others?
h. Did others believe you? Were you blamed?
i. How has your family been? Did this affect them?
j. Has your work/school suffered?
k. Has it affected your sense of competence at work or school?

5. **God/Military/Community/World View**

a. Has your relationship with God or your faith been affected?
b. Has this changed the way you think of the military? How?
c. How has this changed your perception of other people?
d. Of the world? Has your view of the world changed? (Optimistic to pessimistic, naïve to cynical)

156 Appendix C

Hopefully these are a basic start. Sometimes victims won't even know what to tell you. Add your own questions and or tailor these questions to the particular issues at hand. It is important that victims can convey the impact the crime against them; you can help.

Index

abduction of children 53, 123–124
access to services 49–51, 91
access to victim 115–116
aggression, socialization to 42–43
Alaggia, R. 101–102
alcohol use and sexual assault 35
allegations of victim 13–14
American Psychological Association (APA) 87
Amish culture 28–29
Antonova, N. 118
Ariely, D. 20–21
attachment to offender, building 72–73
attractiveness of defendants 79
Axsom, D. 36

Bachman, F. 1
Bancroft, Lundy 34
Barnetz, Z. 69
barriers: to disclosures of sexual assault 100; to help-seeking 50–57; to investigation/prosecution of interpersonal violence 14; offenders of sexual assault as 50–52; to resistance of victim 137–139
beliefs and response of victim 18, 29–32
blaming the victim: accusations against 14; alcohol use and 35; Boston Marathon bombing and avoidance of 7; ease of 145; interpersonal violence and 7–8, 10–14; male victims of intimate violence and 89–90; rape myths and 10–13; relationship between offender and victim and 116; in sexual assault 8, 10–13

"blanking out" response of victim 107–108
"blue balls" concept 36
Bonomi, A. E. 109, 122
Boston Marathon bombing (2013) 7

Campbell, R. 8, 107
Catholic Church sexual assault allegations 118
Ceci, S. 79
change, offender's promise of 74–75
Chattoraj, Paramita 27
children: abduction of 53, 123–124; custody of, by offender of sexual assault 123–124; presence/protection of 52–54, 58, 137–138
child victim: case description 1–3; continued contact with offender and 119–120; delayed disclosure and 100–101; disclosure of sexual assault by 101–103; grooming to be a victim and, offender's 77; inability to resist 138–139; nonverbal resistance of 131; parent protection by 63; sibling protection by 53, 106; voir dire questions for 150
Classen, C. C. 40
cognitive biases: confirmation bias 22–23; decision-making of victim and 21; defining 21; familiarity and perception of risk 23–24; fear 24–25; habituation 25; loss aversion 21; personal control 24–25; personalization of risk 25–26; risk 24–25
cognitive response of victim 18, 20–26
collateral consequences for victim 56
confirmation bias 22–23

158 Index

conflict, socialization to 42–43
confusion: about offender 120–121; offender acting normal and creation of 75–76; offender's creation of 75–76, 83; as response of victim 4, 32–38
consent issue 117–118
Constand, Andrea 117
continued contact with offender: access to victim and 115–116; child victim and 119–120; confusion about offender and 120–121; consent issue and 117–118; consequences of disclosure and 117; danger after stopping contact and 123–124; danger can be controlled belief and 122–123; dependency and 119–120; disbelief about offender and 120–121; employment 120; explanations/ excuses for abuse by offender 116–117; interview suggestions for understanding 124–125; love of offender and 122; normal/safe life and, wishing for 121–122; overview 114, 125–126; pets 120; practical issues and 119–120; reasons for not leaving 119–124; relationship as weapon of offender 114–119; residential location 120; resources and, lack of 119; status issues and 118–119; using victim to maintain relationship 117–118; voir dire questions for 151
control: of information about sexual assault by offender 81; personal 24–25; of victim 69
cooperation of victim with offender 70–71, 77
Cortina, Lilia 59
Cosby, Bill 59, 118
counterintuitive behavior 8–10, 15, 145
courage, committing to 143
creative charging in prosecution of sexual assault cases 144
criminal justice system: attractiveness of defendants and 79; challenges of prosecution and 142; cooperation with offender as defense arguments and 70; costs of prosecution 64; defending the victim versus prosecuting the offender and

142–143; "extralegal" factors and 79; myths of sexual assault and 12, 110; recommendations for 143–144; response of victim and successful prosecution and 14–15; victim's experience with 54–57
culture: Amish 28–29; jury perception of victim and 27–28; masculinity and 87; Mexican American 27; response of victim and 18, 26–29

danger: after stopping contact with offender 123–124; control of, belief in 122–123
de Becker, G. 73
deceptive behavior of offender after disclosure of sexual assault 82–83
decision-making of victim: cognitive biases and 21; exhaustion from intense fear and 20; questions for understanding 147–148; vulnerability caused by 38–39
defense cascade 20
delayed disclosure of victim 12, 100–101
denial by offender of sexual assault 82
dependency and continued contact with offender 119–120
depersonalization response of victim 107–108
direct addressing of issues in prosecution of sexual assault 143
disbelief about offender 120–121
disclosures of sexual assault: barriers to 100; by child victim 101–103; consequences of 117; delayed 12, 100–101; as evidence of sexual assault 2; inconsistencies in 98–99, 108; interactional component of 102–104; interviewer's behavior and 103–104, 108; knowledge of victim and, increased 105–106; memory and 98–100, 106–108; offender's removal and 106; open-ended versus close-ended questions and 103; opportunities for 104–105; overview 97–98, 110–111; physical injury or other needs of victim and 105; process over details and 99–100; protection of other victims and 106; recantation and 108–109; scrutiny of 97; secondary

Index   159

victimization as result of 109–110; social support and 104–105; telling process and 101–104; test balloons and 102; time and, passing of 103; trauma and 104, 106–108; triggers for 104–106; types of 101–102; voir dire questions for 150–151
dissociation response of victim 40–41, 104, 107
domestic violence: incidence of 101; law enforcement experiences of victim and 55; myths about 10–13; offender's creating victim's reputation and 81–82; victim 106
Dugard, Jaycee 54

education about sexual assault 11, 143–144
Edwards, K. 129
egocentric needs, using against victim 80
Einstein, Albert 142
emotional impact of fear 19
emotional response of victim 18–20
erection response of male victims of intimate violence 87–89
escape opportunities 54, 135
evidence-based investigation of sexual assault 144
exhaustion from intense fear 20
experience of victim with offender, past 78–79
expert witnesses in prosecution of sexual assault 143
external factors impacting victim's response: access to services 49–51; barriers to help-seeking during offenses 50–57; children/witnesses, presence/protection of 52–54, 58; criminal justice system 54–57; escape opportunities 54; law enforcement experiences 54–57; overview 49, 64–65; parents, protection of 63; pressure to return to normal 64; prosecution costs 64; reporting consequences 57–60; societal messages 60–61; support system, victim's 61–63; third parties 57–59, 63; time passed since offense 63

Facebook 62
failure to identify sexual assault 32–37

familiarity and perception of risk 23–24
fear: of blame 89; cognitive bias and 24–25; emotional impact of 19; exhaustion from intense 20; Gardner's analysis of 23–25; of penalization/retaliation 43–45, 59–60; perceived risk and 23–24; physiological impact of 19–20; as response of victim 4, 19–20
fight response of victim 136–137
financial costs of prosecution 64
Flåm, A. M. 102
flight response of victim 134–136
Flood, M. 28
force in sexual assault, absence of 35–37
freezing response of victim 20, 132–134
"friending" victim, offender's 115

Gardener, Daniel 23–25
gender expectations 28, 31
gender orientation see LGBTQ issues and sexual assault
gender roles and socialization to aggression/conflict 42
Gift of Fear, The (de Becker) 73
"gold diggers," victims as 14, 80
Grietens, H. 102
Grills-Taquechel, A. 36
"grooming" victim to be victim 76–77, 103
guilt response of victim 37–38
Gunnell, J. 79

habituation 25
Haugstevedt, E. 102
helplessness response of victim 4, 40
help-seeking: access to services and 49–51, 91; barriers to 50–57; physical injury and 90–91
history of sexual assault, prior 39–42, 138
hope, offender's creation of 74–75

information available about sexual assault, offender's control of 81
interactional component of disclosures 102–104
internal factors impacting victim's response: alcohol use 35; beliefs 18, 29–32; cognitive 18, 20–26;

confusion 32–37; culture 18, 26–29; emotional 18–20; fear of penalization 43–45; force/violence, absence of 35–37; guilt 37–38; history of sexual assault, prior 39–42; overview 18, 45; relationship to offender 33–35; religion 26–29; self-blame 37–38; shame 37–38; socialization to aggression/conflict 42–43; spiritual beliefs 26–29; values 18, 29–32; vulnerability caused by victim's decisions 38–39
interpersonal violence: barriers to investigation/prosecution of 14; blaming the victim and 7–8, 10–14; case descriptions 1–3; common sense about 12; compliance and 97; confusion created by 4; fear created by 4; helplessness created by 4; investigation/prosecution of 14–15; Mexican American culture and 27; prosecution challenges and 142; *see also* response of victim; sexual assault
interviewer's behavior 103–104, 108
interviewing victims for sentencing 154–156
interview suggestions for understanding continued contact with offender 124–125
intimate partner violence (IPV) 11, 110; *see also* interpersonal violence
investigation/prosecution of interpersonal violence 14–15
isolation, social 101

Jackson, Michael 122
judge's perceptions of sexual assault victim 143
jury's perceptions of sexual assault victim 28, 143
"just world" concept 30–31

Kahn, A. 40
Katz, C. 69
knowledge of victim and disclosure, increased 105–106
Kristiansson, V. 9

law enforcement 54–57; *see also* criminal justice system
learned helplessness response of victim 41

Leaving Neverland (documentary) 122
Lerner, M. 30
LGBTQ issues and sexual assault 51, 54–55, 90
Littleton, H. 36
Logan, T. 123
Long, J. 9
loss/loss aversion 21, 60
Lowe, M. 89
lust, concept of overpowering 36
Lyon, T. 129

McDonald, E. 11
McKeever, N. 88
male victims of intimate violence: access to services and 91; blaming the victim and 89–90; erection response and 87–89; fear of blame and 89; incidence of 86; LGBTQ issues and 90; masculinity and 86–87; minimization of sexual assault and 90–91; overview 85–86, 91–92; reporting of, low number of 85; sexual dysfunction of 88; shame of 89; societal messages and 86–87; stigma of 89
Mallios, C. 9
manliness and male victims of intimate violence 86–87
marital rape 32–33
Marsalis, Jeffrey 121
masculinity and male victims of intimate violence 86–87
memory: complexity of 98; disclosures of sexual assault and 98–100, 106–108; general issues 98–100; inconsistencies and 98–99; trauma and 104, 106–108
mental health issues 72
Mexican American culture and interpersonal violence 27
Michigan State University 8
military victim 106
myths about sexual assault 10–15, 31–32, 88, 110

Nassar, Larry 118
National Crime Victimization Survey 8, 86
National Domestic Violence Hotline survey 55
needs of victim and disclosure, increased 105

Index 161

nice behavior of offender toward victim 73–74
NIMBY (Not in My Back Yard) concept 26
nonintuitive behavior *see* counterintuitive behavior
nonverbal victim resistance 131–132
normal: confusion about offender acting 75–76; pressure to return to 64; wishing for life that safe and 121–122

offender of sexual assault: access to victim by 115–116; attachment to victim, building 72–73; as barrier to help-seeking 50–52; change and, promise of 74–75; confusion about 120–121; confusion created by 75–76, 83; consequences of reporting and 57–59; controlling victim and 69; cooperation of victim, getting 70–71, 77; counterintuitive behavior of 145; custody of children and 123–124; deceptive behavior after disclosure of sexual assault 82–83; denial by 82; disbelief about 120–121; experience with victim, past 78–79; explanations/excuses for abuse by 116–117; focus on by prosecution 143; "friending" victim by 115; "grooming"/preparing victim to be victim 76–77, 103; hope and, creating 74–75; influence of 145; information available about sexual assault, controlling 81; love of by victim 122; nice behavior toward victim and 73–74; public persona, creation of 80–81; questions for behavior of 148–149; relationship to 33–35, 37, 43, 114–119; removal of and disclosure 106; reputation of 80–81; reputation of victim and, creating/setting up for retaliation 81–82; retaliation by 43–45, 59–60, 81–82; status issues of 118–119; violent 77; voir dire questions for behavior of 152–153; vulnerability of victim, exposing/exploiting 71–72; *see also* continued contact with offender
offender's influence on community: deceptive behavior after disclosure

of sexual assault 82–83; information available about sexual assault, controlling 81; overview 79–80, 83–84; public persona, creation of 80–81; reputation of victim, creating/setting up for retaliation 81–82
offender's influence on victim's behavior: attachment to victim, building 72–73; change, promising 74–75; confusion caused by acting normal 75–76; cooperation of victim, getting 70–71, 77; "grooming"/preparing victim to be victim 76–77, 103; hope, creating 74–75; nice behavior toward victim 73–74; overview 68–70, 83–84; past experience with offender 78–79; vulnerability of victim, exposing/exploiting 71–72
opportunities for disclosures 104–105

Page, A. D. 109
Pandher, Gurdeep 74
Paquette, D. 7
parents, child victim's protection of 63
Payne, B. 110
Pease, B. 28
penalization, fear of 43–45, 59–60
perpetrator of sexual assault *see* offender of sexual assault
physical injury and help-seeking/ disclosure 90–91, 105
physiological impact of fear 19–20
Policastro, C. 110
post-traumatic stress disorder (PTSD) 3, 62, 104, 133
"Power of Hope, The" (Pandher) 74
practical issues of continued contact with offender 119–120
Predictably Irrational (Ariely) 20–21
pressure to return to normal 64
prosecution of sexual assault: attractiveness of defendants and 79; barriers to 14; challenges 142; costs, financial 64; courage and, committing to 143; creative charging and 144; direct addressing of issues in 143; evidence-based investigation and 144; expert witnesses in, using 143; judge/jury in, education about sexual assault 143; offender behavior questions

148–149; offender and, focusing on 143; opposition's comments during 145; questions for, basic 144–145; response of victim and successful 14–15; self-care and 144; self-education about sexual assault and 144; victim decision-making/experiences questions and 147–148; voir dire questions and, sample 150–153; "why" questions in, avoiding 143; "winning" and, reframing 143
protection: of children 52–54, 58; of other victims 106; of parents 63; of sibling 53
Protection From Abuse (PFA) order 29
public persona of offender, creation of 80–81

RAINN (Rape Abuse Incest National Network) statistics 56, 59
rape: blaming the victim and 10–14; "blue balls" concept and 36; "culture" 60–61; lust and, concept of overpowering 36; male 85, 88; marital 32–33; myths about 10–11, 13, 31–32, 88, 110; response of victim to 12–13; "scripts" 13, 22, 24, 31–32; *see also* male victims of intimate violence; sexual assault
"rape paralysis" 20
recantation of sexual assault disclosure 108–109
recommendations for criminal justice system 143–144
Reed, Dan 122
Reitsema, A. 102
relationship to offender: sexual assault and 33–35, 37, 43; as weapon of offender 114–119, 142
religion and response of victim 26–29
reporting sexual assault: consequences of 57–60; failure to 32–37; loss and 60; by male victims 85; offender and 57–59; retaliation and 59–60; statistics on filing 8, 56; time passed between offense and 63; voir dire questions for 151–152
reputation: of offender 80–81; of victim, creating/setting up for retaliation 81–82

resistance of victim: barriers to 137–139; children and, protection of 137–139; feezing response 132–134; fight response 136–137; flight response 134–136; history of abuse and, prior 138; inability to resist and 138–139; nonverbal 131–132; overview 128–129, 139–140; types of 129; understanding 128–129; verbal 129–131
response of victim: beliefs and 18, 29–32; "blanking out" 107–108; cognitive 18, 20–26; confusion 4, 32–38; as counterintuitive behavior, perception of 8–10, 15, 145; culture and 18, 26–29; delayed disclosure 12; depersonalization 107–108; dissociation 40–41, 104, 107; emotional 18–20; factors influencing 15, 18, 20–21, 45; fear 4, 19–20; fear of penalization 43–45; fight 136–137; flight 134–136; freezing 20, 132–134; guilt 37–38; helplessness 4, 40; importance of understanding 4, 14–15, 145; individual 15, 144–145; "just world" concept and 30–31; learned helplessness 41; overview 15; prosecution and, successful 14–15; to rape 12–13; religion and 26–29; retrospective evaluation 39; self-blame 37–38, 88; shame 37–38, 89; spiritual beliefs and 26–29; unanticipated 10; values and 18, 29–32; *see also* external factors impacting victim's response; internal factors impacting victim's response; offender's influence on victim's behavior
retaliation against victim 43–45, 59–60, 81–82
retrospection 39
revictimization by law enforcement 54–57
Riccardi, P. 87
Rice, Ray 110
risk: cognitive bias and 24–25; familiarity and perception of 23–24; faulty perception of 23–24; fear and perceived 23–24; personalization of 25–26; voluntariness factor and 24–25

Rogers, P. 89
rural areas and sexual assault 51

Salam, M. 120–121
Sandusky, Jerry 118
Science of Fear, The (Gardner) 23
secondary victimization as result of disclosure 109–110
self-blame response of victim 37–38, 88
self-care in prosecuting sexual assault cases 144
self-education about sexual assault 144
services, access to 49–51, 91
sex-trafficking 56
sexual assault: access to services and 49–51; acquittal rates 11; alcohol use and 35; blaming the victim and 8, 10–13; case attrition 8; case descriptions 1–3; confusion about 32–38; education about 11, 143–144; evidence-based investigation of 144; evidence of 2; facts 13–14; force in, absence of 35–37; guilt and 37–38; history of, prior 39–42, 138; identifying, failure to 32–37; incidence 8; information about, offender's controlling of 81; LGBTQ issues and 51, 54–55, 90; in military 106; minimization of 90–91; myths about 10–15, 31–32, 88, 110; neurobiology of 106–107; private nature of 18, 52, 121; recantation of disclosure of 108–109; relationship to offender and 33–35, 37, 43; reports filed 8, 56; in rural areas 51; self-blame and 37–38; shame and 37–38, 89; socialization to aggression/ conflict and 42–43, 86–87; societal messages about 60–61; stigma of 54–55, 89; time passed between reporting and 63; violence in, absence of 35–37; vulnerability caused by victim's decisions and 38–39; weapons used in 13; *see also* disclosures of sexual assault; offender's influence on victim's behavior; rape; reporting sexual assault; response of victim
Sexual Assault Nurse Examiners survey 55

sexual dysfunction of male victims of intimate violence 88
sexual harassment 59–60
sexual orientation *see* LGBTQ issues and sexual assault
shame response of victim 37–38, 89
sibling, child victim's protection of 53, 106
Simmons, C. 30
Smart, Elizabeth 54
social isolation 101
socialization to aggression/conflict 42–43
social media for supporting victims 62
social support of victim 61–63, 104–105
societal messages about sexual assault 60–61, 86–87
spiritual beliefs and response of victim 26–29
status issues of offender 118–119
stereotyping, gender 10
stigma of sexual assault 54–55, 89
Stolzenberg, S. 129
support system of victim 61–63, 104–105

telling process 101–104
"test balloons" 102–103
Thinking and Deciding (Baron) 21
third parties 57–59, 63
time passed between sexual assault and reporting 63
tonic immobility 20
trauma: disclosures of sexual assault and 104, 106–108; memory and 104, 106–108; neurobiology of 106–107; post-traumatic stress disorder and 3, 62, 104, 133

U.S. Bureau of Justice Statistics 10

values and response of victim 18, 29–32
verbal victim resistance 129–131
victim *see* response of victim
victim blaming *see* blaming the victim
violence in sexual assault, absence of 35–37
voir dire questions, sample 150–153
voluntariness factor and risk 24–25
vulnerability: offender's identifying/ exploiting of 71–72; victim's decisions as causing 38–39

Walker, R. 123
weakness implied with term "victim" 38–39
Weinstein, Harvey 59, 118
whistleblowers, retaliation towards 59
Why Does He do That (Bancroft) 34

"why" questions in prosecution of sexual assault, avoiding 143–144
"winning" in prosecution of sexual assault, reframing 143
witnesses, presence/protection of 52–54